The Assault on Trade Union Freedoms

Network Foundation for Educational Publishing

Network Foundation is a voluntary membership foundation. General policy and overall objectives are established by the membership and administered by an elected Executive Committee. An Advisory Board, appointed by the Executive from the ranks of the membership, advises on all publishing decisions.

Foundation Objectives:

1. To facilitate the development of a healthy and responsible Canadian-controlled post-secondary book publishing sector.

2. To assist in the production, dissemination and popularizing of innovative texts and other educational meaterials for people at all levels of learnings.

3. To develop more varied sources for critical works in the Humanities and Social Sciences.

4. To expand the readership for Canadian academic works beyond a select body of scholars.

5. To encourage the academic community to create books on Canadian topics for the community at large.

6. To develop works that will contribute to public information and debate on issues of historical and contemporary concern, thereby improving standards of education and public participation.

The Network Basics Series, one of the Foundation's activities, provides inexpensive books of the leading edge of research and debate to students and the general public.

This Network Basic is published by Garamond Press. Please direct all enquiries to 163 Neville Park Boulevard, Toronto, Ontario, M4E 3P7.

The Assault on
Trade Union Freedoms

From Consent to Coercion Revisited

Leo Panitch
Donald Swartz

Garamond Press
Toronto
A Network Basics Book

A publication of Garamond Press

Garamond Press
67A Portland Street
Toronto, Ontario M5V 2M9

Cover design: Peter McArthur
Cover photo: Kolley, *The Globe and Mail*, August 28, 1987
Typesetting: LaserGraphics, Halifax

Printed and bound in Canada

Canadian Cataloguing in Publication Data

Panitch, Leo, 1945-
   The assault on trade union freedoms

(Network basics series)
Rev. ed.
First ed. published under title: From consent to coercion.
Includes bibliographical references.
ISBN 0-920059-70-8 (trade ed.) — ISBN 0-920059-66-X (student ed.).

1. Collective bargaining - Canada - History.
I. Swartz, Donald, 1945-   . II. Title. III. Title: From consent to coercion. IV. Series

HD6524.P36 1988   331.89'0971   C88-093286-4

Dedication

From *Consent to Coercion* was dedicated to the memory of those who laboured to build the working class movement in Canada. We would like to dedicate *The Assault on Trade Union Freedoms: From Consent to Coercion Revisited* to those in the labour movement who have borne the brunt of that assault and struggled most tenaciously against it, above all, to Jean Claude Parrot and the members of the Canadian Union of Postal Workers.

Contents

Preface

Today's free trade debate is as much about democracy as it is about national sovereignty. Societies defined as "free" in the sense of free trade and free enterprise have often been, and often are today, societies in which the freedoms of workers and those who advance the interests of workers are suppressed. In the midst of the "free trade" debate, we hope this book helps to inject a clearer awareness that what really confronts Canadians today is the actual meaning of the word "free" as our society approaches the twenty-first century. We need to ask ourselves whether "free" pertains only to the freedom of those who *do* business or whether it pertains also to the freedom of the majority of Canadians who don't *do* business, but rather, work for those who own businesses, or who work for governments, which increasingly act as if they were businesses themselves.

Over the past year, fundamental issues concerning the nature of Canadian democracy and the state have come to the fore with the discovery that a federal government agency routinely spied on peace groups, radical political parties and trade unions. In April, 1987, the Supreme Court ruled that the *Charter of Rights and Freedom*'s guarantee of freedom of association did not include the right to strike. Canadian Crown corporations developed elaborate schemes for deploying strike breakers against public employees. Canadian governments, from 1985-87, used back-to-work legislation more frequently than ever before to remove from workers the right to strike provided in general legislation, even as that general legislation was amended restrictively in a growing number of jurisdictions. Moreover, in 1987, the federal government actually interfered directly with the right of postal workers to choose their own union representatives freely and to speak out openly against the Canada Post's privatization of postal services. The picture on the cover of this book of police in riot gear on the steps of Parliament, massed against a demonstration by railway workers in August 1987, was but one graphic symbol of a rising number of incidents over the past few years where police confronted groups of workers protesting the attacks on their freedom of association. We can recognize in the police batons an almost inevitable, and always ugly, social consequence when basic rights and freedoms are denied.

The origins of this book go back to 1982, when controversy still swirled around the Trudeau Government's introduction of its "6 and 5" public sector wage-controls programme. This programme initiated a process whereby almost one-third of Canada's organized workers lost their right to strike for two-to-three years. In October of that year, we argued in a paper that this measure heralded the closing of an era of free collective bargaining and the shift toward a more coercive, less consensual system of state-labour relations. The paper was widely noted, with various versions of the argument published inside and outside the labour movement. In 1984, Garamond Press asked us to update the paper and extend our discussion of trends in the provinces. This appeared in the monograph, *From Consent to Coercion*, in the spring of 1985.

In view of that monograph's relatively wide use among students and trade unionists, and continuing developments which seemed to confirm our argument, Garamond suggested in the summer of 1987 that we prepare a revised edition. Before we finished documenting and analysing the relevant material, it became clear to us that we could not just revise and up-date the earlier work. We were in the process of producing virtually a new book on the post-controls period after 1984. We present to the reader, therefore, a book with two parts. Part One, entitled "From Consent to Coercion," contains the revised versions of the two substantive chapters of the earlier monograph. Part Two, entitled "The Assault on Trade Union Freedoms," contains two new chapters covering the 1984 to 1987 period. We have also added a completely revised and much expanded concluding chapter.

This last chapter, more an analysis of the state of the contemporary labour movement than a conventional conclusion, reflects our sense of the far-reaching implications for working people of the consolidation of a new era of coercion, and for the changes unions are already undergoing — and will still need to undergo — in developing the capacity to withstand and transcend it. In the original preface to From *Consent to Coercion*, we remarked on the lack of sensitivity among Canadians regarding the abrogation of fundamental union freedoms, above all, the right to strike. Now, there is welcome evidence this is changing. As we point out in the concluding chapter, 1987 opinion poll data show no less than 68 per cent of Canadians had come to the view that workers *should* have the right to strike. Moreover, there has been considerable public sympathy in recent years for those workers who have tenaciously defended their rights to the point of defying repressive laws. As we write, eleven thousand nurses in Alberta are engaging in an illegal strike, despite having had their right to do so abrogated four years ago. If the developments we discuss in this book are cause for concern, we are heartened by recent changes in the labour movement, and more broadly, which suggest a greater willingness and capacity to resist these developments.

We have many acknowledgements to make. The Carleton School of Public Administration's invitation to present a paper at a conference on "the future of public sector industrial relations" was the impetus for a project that has occupied much of our attention over the ensuing six years. (The proceedings of that conference, including our paper, were published under the auspices of the Institute for Research on Public Policy in a book edited by Gene Swimmer and Mark Thompson entitled, *Conflict or Compromise*) A somewhat revised version of that paper also appeared in *Labour/Le Travail*, 13, 1984. When this was expanded into the monograph, *From Consent to Coercion*, Greg Albo's research assistance had been invaluable to us. The same must now be said for Chris Boyle, who worked with us researching Part Two of this book. Few authors could have been as fortunate in having such capable and inspired researchers. Thanks to the generous financial assistance of Carleton and York Universities, we were able to provide both of these outstanding students of labour and the state with some recompense. We would like to thank Peter Saunders and Errol Sharpe at Garamond Press for their encouragement; as well, we thank Carmen Palumbo for his outstanding editorial work on the manuscript and Sharon Nelson for seeing to the speedy preparation and publication of the book. We also could not have managed without the benefit of discussions and criticisms, as well as considerable help, from many other friends and colleagues in the universities and the labour movement. In this regard, special thanks are due to Harry Arthurs, Amy Bartholemew, Geoff Bickerton, Linda Briskin, Sam Gindin, Harry Glasbeek, Ian Green, John Laing, Gil Levine, Gene Swimmer, Rosemary Warskett and Reg Whitaker. And finally, to Melanie Panitch and Jane Swartz, and our children, who provided support and encouragement when it was most needed.

Leo Panitch
Donald Swartz
February 1988

CHAPTER 1

Introduction

If every State tends to create and maintain a certain type of civilization and of citizen ... then the Law will be its instrument for this purpose.... It operates according to plan, urges, incites, solicits, and "punishes;" ... The Law is the repressive and negative aspect of the entire positive, civilising aspect of the State.

Antonio Gramsci [1]

Just take a look at what happened to Lech Walesa in Communist Poland and take a look at what happened to Fraser March in Democratic Canada ... I think that would tell you something of the problems that trade unions have in trying to represent their members.

Fraser March [2]

The era of free collective bargaining began with the federal government's 1944 Order-in-Council 1003. This Order-in-Council established legal recognition of the rights of private sector workers across Canada to organize, to bargain collectively, and to strike, and backed these rights with state sanctions against employers who refused to recognize and bargain with trade unions. In 1948, Privy Council 1003 was superseded by the *Industrial Relations Disputes Investigation Act*, giving these rights a "permanent" legislative basis for private sector workers under federal jurisdiction. Broadly similar legislation was adopted by the provinces for private sector (and municipal) workers in their jurisdiction, with notable delay only by Quebec. These legally established rights have been universally seen, and not least by the Canadian trade union movement itself, as the point at which Canada extended democracy to include "free collective bargaining" and finally effectively conformed with the General Principles enunciated in 1919 in the Constitution of the International Labour Organization (ILO): "First. The guiding principle ... that labour should not be regarded as a commodity or article of commerce; Second. The right of association for all lawful purposes by the employed as well as by the employers." Despite continuing exclusions and limitations on free trade unionism in Canada, it was widely assumed, in a way that was typical of the reformist ideology that predominated in labour relations in the post-war era, that there would be steady if slow progress toward the ever fuller realization of trade union rights. The reforms achieved in the 1940s were thought to be irreversible and cumulative. Such a world view inevitably tends to outlive the social realities which gave rise to it. The social realities of the 1980s may have finally put it to rest.

It is one of the greater ironies of the 1980s that as the Canadian state finally moved to formally guarantee liberal democratic freedoms in an indigenous constitution, so has it simultaneously moved toward restricting those elements of liberal democracy that specifically pertain to workers' freedoms. Canada's new Constitution with its *Charter of Rights and Freedoms*, notably, excluded the right to strike from its list of fundamental freedoms. It might have been thought that in guaranteeing the right to freedom of association, the federal and provincial governments were implicitly recognizing the right to strike alone makes workers' rights to freedom of association viable. However, within months of the proclamation of the Constitution, the right to strike was abrogated for over one million of the 3.5 million organized workers in Canada, through a series of federal and provincial legislative measures.

The most important of these measures, because it clearly symbolized the significance of the Charter's silences on the right to strike, was the federal *Public Sector Compensation Restraint Act* (Bill C-124), introduced in June 1982. This Act tended to be treated as imposing a two-year period of statutory wage restraint on federal employees in conformity with the slogan of "6 and 5." But the Act did much more; it completely suppressed the right to bargain and strike for all those public employees covered by the legislation. Most provinces quickly followed suit. Ontario introduced Bill 179 which not only followed the federal Act in form but was even broader in scope. In Quebec and British Columbia, events took a somewhat different and even more menacing course. The Parti Québecois government of Quebec with Bill 105 decreed, unilaterally, one- to three-year collective agreements for public sector workers, thereby pre-empting their right to strike. The Social Credit government in British Columbia went a great deal further with a range of legislative measures, including Bills 3, 11 and 50, to permanently restrict union rights. In all of these, and the other measures which will be examined, the *form* of free collective bargaining was preserved while its *substance* was dramatically curtailed.

These measures were often presented initially as "temporary," as merely "suspending" free collective bargaining. Yet this was a case where the old French saying—*c'est seulement le provisoire qui dure* (it's only the provisional that lasts)—had particular merit. For these "temporary" measures were part of a long-term trend, which included the adoption of the statutory incomes policy in 1975; the jailing of prominent union leaders from the leaders of the Quebec Common

Front, in the early 1970s, to Fraser March, the leader of the Newfoundland public employees, in the mid-1980s; the increased designation of public sector workers as "essential," thereby removing their right to strike; and the growing use of back-to-work legislation which suspends a group of workers' right to strike when they actually exercise it.

Most industrial relations experts view the restrictions on workers' trade union rights introduced in the early 1980s mainly as temporary and conjunctural. In a recent comment on this period of legislated controls for public sector workers, two such observers concluded that "the long-term impact on collective bargaining of the 1982 round of wage restrictions does not appear substantial," and the "major changes of the 1980s — public sector wage controls or restrictions on interest arbitrators appear to represent a political response to public issues of the day rather than an attempt to eliminate disfunctions or problems in the system".[3] This statement of faith in the permanence of reform — echoed in another expert's facile reference to "the inherent dynamism of the institution of collective bargaining"[4]—is astonishingly myopic. Rather more insightful was the view expressed by Donald Carter in 1985 that, with the growing movement toward deregulation of the private sector and continued fiscal pressures in the public sphere, "it would be premature to predict that we have seen the end of legislated wage restraint in the public sector."[5]

Developments in the legislative regime governing industrial relations in Canada during the post-controls period hardly suggest a return to the *status quo ante* but rather a continued movement away from the principles characteristic of the post-war era of "free collective bargaining," and toward the institutionalization of "permanent exceptionalism." Despite the fact that continued high unemployment and moderate inflation have combined to limit union wage increases to their lowest in twenty-five years, the process of legislative restructuring of the collective bargaining system, involving attacks on the very foundations of organized workers' power within it, has continued through the 1980s.

The ongoing efforts of capital to restructure itself, in the face of the enduring economic crisis and the heightened international competition integral to it, has entailed continued employer demands for new concessions in wages and work rules from workers. Precisely because Canadian workers—much more than their American counterparts—have willingly resorted to lengthy strikes to defend their historic achievements, Ottawa and the provinces began to broaden their powers to intervene in collective bargaining in the private as well as the public sector. This has involved new measures allowing the state to limit or suspend strike action by workers, while providing numerous mechanisms to undermine their bargaining power through interference in internal union affairs. Combined with new restrictions on picketing and secondary strike action by unions, while enhancing employers' access to non-union labour, such measures essentially function to weaken the ability of workers to "take wages out of competition." Therefore, without destroying the *formal structure* of collective bargaining, governments have made further and avowedly *permanent* encroachments on workers' collective freedoms within that structure.

What we appear to witness in the 1980s is the end of the era of free collective bargaining in Canada. The era being left behind is one in which the state and capital relied, more than before World War II, on obtaining the consent of workers generally, and unions in particular, to act as subordinates in Canada's capitalist democracy. The era we have entered marks a return, albeit in quite different conditions, to the state and capital relying more openly on coercion—on force and on fear—to secure that subordination. This is *not* to suggest that coercion was in any sense absent from the post-war era or that coercion is about to become the only, or even always the dominant, factor in labour relations. But there *is* a changing conjuncture in the Canadian political economy, and it marks a change in the form in which coercion and consent are related to one another, a change significant enough to demarcate a new era.

We trace in Part I this shift from an era of consent to an era of coercion. Chapter Two examines the contradictions and limitations contained within the reforms of the 1940s and goes on to show that the evolution of labour legislation in the following decades did not correspond to the gradualist assumptions of reformist ideology. "Industrial citizenship" was extended to federal and provincial government workers only under the specific economic and political conditions of the 1960s, and even then, in restricted form. Chapter Three demonstrates that as these conditions faded, the labour relations regime in Canada turned toward "permanent exceptionalism" whereby rights established in the general legislation of the 1940s and 1960s were increasingly removed, on an *ad hoc* basis, from particular groups of workers who sought to exercise them, and eventually, from large segments of the working class altogether for a "temporary" period through statutory wage controls. Part II is concerned with the more permanent nature of the attack on trade union freedoms in the post-controls period of 1985 to 1987. Chapter Four documents the growing number of complaints by Canadian unions to the ILO regarding governmental violations of freedom of association, and follows the long battle through the courts in Canada over the question of whether the guarantee of freedom of association in the *Charter of Rights and Freedoms* would be juridically construed to include the right to strike. Chapter Five then examines the consolidation of this new era of coercion under the Mulroney Government at the federal level and the growing, permanent restrictions placed on trade unions in both the public and private sectors at the provincial level. We also investigate there such instances of reform as can be found in the new era, and find that they are limited and constrained. Finally, the concluding chapter analyses the condition of the labour movement in this era and its response to the assault on union freedoms, and it discusses Canadian labour's capacity to cope with and transcend the challenges it confronts today.

PART ONE

CHAPTER 2

The Era of Free Collective Bargaining

It is the pattern in all countries that, as soon as the bourgeoisie reconciles itself to the fact that trade unionism is here to stay, it ceases to denounce the institution as a subversive evil that has to be rooted out with fire and sword in order to defend God, country and motherhood, and turns instead to the next line of defence: domesticating the unions, housebreaking them, and fitting them into the national family as one of the tame cats.[1]

Hal Draper

The social relations under which capitalist production takes place embody a structural antagonism between employers and employees. Since the employment contract gives the employer, as the purchaser of labour time, the right to determine what work is done by employees, exercising this right involves the use of power. In turn, workers have historically recognized that collective organization and the threat of collective withdrawal of labour are necessary to advance their interests *vis-à-vis* the employer. Both formally free actors in the capitalist labour market, the employer and employee seek to establish their interests, ideologically and legally, in terms of rights the state recognizes: the rights of property and managerial prerogative on the one hand, and on the other, the right of association and the right to strike.

The evolution of liberal capitalist societies into liberal democratic societies is conventionally understood in terms of the institution of mass suffrage. However, the distinction between a democratic or authoritarian capitalist regime is never only one of mass suffrage. It is equally, indeed in some cases more clearly, a distinction which rests on the absence or presence of freedom of association. The long struggle of the working classes for political representation within the state system, was matched through the nineteenth and twentieth centuries by an equally long struggle against the legal prohibition of the right to free association for wage labour. Liberal democracy not only brought the working class into the representative system on the basis of individual, universalistic criteria; it also involved the state's recognition of the collective, class-specific organization of labour, the trade unions, as legitimate representatives of workers. Moreover, the independence of trade unions from direct interference by the state itself, had to be established.

From Coercion to Consent

Prior to 1872 in Canada, trade unions were *per se* illegal, defined as "combinations" in the "restraint of trade." The *Trade Unions Act* of 1872 did not grant positive rights to unions, but only granted trade unions and their members a certain immunity from criminal prosecution.[2] This did not mean that from this point forward, the state acted to promote union organization or collective bargaining. On the contrary, capital's right to continue to resist unionization, in the succeeding decades, was the chief focus of "industrial relations." The state's extensive use of force in defence of this right became a hallmark of Canadian labour history, with the deployment of the Royal North West Mounted Police against the workers in the 1919 Winnipeg general strike symbolizing the coercive role of the state. To be sure, the Royal Commission on the Relations of Labour and Capital of 1889, the establishment of the Department of Labour in 1900, and the *Industrial Disputes Investigation Act* (IDIA) of 1907 were all indicative of the state's attempts to moderate and contain class conflict. But even the most progressive manifestation of the ruling ideology *vis-à-vis* the "labour problem" in the first decades of the century (as enunciated by Mackenzie King, while the first Deputy Minister of Labour, and later, the first Minister of Labour, well before he became Liberal leader and Prime Minister—with an interim stint as Rockefeller's industrial relations consultant) rested on a blatantly political distinction between "legitimate" and "illegitimate" trade unionism. And even for unions regarded as fundamentally oriented toward class collaboration, and hence as "legitimate," the 1907 Act, and state practices under its rubric, were filled with coercive implications and restrictions on freedom of association, including the right to strike. In the characteristic fashion of the Canadian state until the 1940s, the Act was directed "toward the *ad hoc* suspension of hostilities," in the context of "a generalised defence of private property rights by the capitalist state."[3]

In the 1940s, the state turned away from *ad hoc* coercive and conciliation mechanisms *vis-à-vis* workers' struggles for union recognition and began to recognize the principle of freedom of association for workers. It was only with the Privy Council Order 1003, a wartime measure, that a comprehensive, stable policy emerged favouring union recognition and free collective bargaining. The tenor of this new policy was graphically captured in Justice Rand's famous 1946 ruling on union security:

> Any modification of relations between the parties here concerned must be made within the framework of a society whose economic life has

private enterprise as its dynamic. And it is the accommodation of that principle of action with evolving notions of social justice in the area of industrial mass production, that becomes the problem for decision.

Certain declarations of policy of both Dominion and Provincial legislatures furnish me with the premises from which I must proceed. In most of the Provinces, and by Dominion war legislation, the social desirability of the organisation of workers and of collective bargaining where employees seek them has been written into laws.... The corollary from it is that the labour unions should become strong in order to carry on the functions for which they are intended. This is machinery devised to adjust, toward an increasing harmony, the interests of capital, labour and public in the production of goods and services which our philosophy accepts as part of the good life; it is to secure industrial civilization within a framework of labour-employer constitutional law based on a rational economic and social doctrine....

In industry, capital must in the long run be looked upon as occupying a dominant position. It is in some respects at greater risk than labour; but as industry becomes established, these risks change inversely. Certainly the predominance of capital against individual labour is unquestionable; and in mass relations, hunger is more imperious than passed dividends.

Against the consequence of that, as the history of the past century has demonstrated, the power of organised labour, the necessary co-partner of capital, must be available to redress the balance of what is called social justice; the just protection of all interests in an activity which the social order approves and encourages.[4]

It must be stressed that this new era in labour relations did not evolve suddenly from the minds of legislators, judges, and industrial relations experts. Nor had capitalists miraculously been transformed into far-sighted social philosophers (as Rand's ruling against the Ford Motor Company itself attests). Rather, the labour legislation of the 1940s was a product of an heretofore unparalleled shift in the balance of class forces in Canadian society. Beginning in the mid-1930s, and increasing with intensity under national mobilization for war and the return of full employment in the early 1940s, Canada witnessed an unprecedented tide of sustained and comprehensive working class mobilization and politicization. As the prominent historian H.A. Logan stated, the "trade union world seethed with discontent over the injustices resulting from the refusal of both private and government corporations to bargain collectively."[5] In 1943, one out of every three trade union members was engaged in strike action, a proportion only exceeded in 1919.[6] Union membership, just as significantly, grew rapidly, doubling between 1940 and 1944.

This industrial militancy was politically punctuated by the dramatic rise of the Cooperative Commonwealth Federation (CCF) in the opinion polls, by Communist and CCF victories in the 1943 federal by-elections, as well as the rather hasty conversion of the Liberal and Conservative parties to reforms along the lines of the Keynesian-welfare state. While the threat of any direct political challenge had largely evaporated by 1945—as evidenced in the Ontario and

TABLE I
Union Membership in Canada 1940-48

	Membership (,000s)	% of Non-agricultural Workforce
1940	362	17.3
1944	724	24.3
1948	978	30.3

SOURCE: Labour Organisation in Canada (Ottawa: 1975) pp. 28-9.

federal elections of that year—the industrial militancy did not pass away. The temporary industrial relations reform initiated by Privy Council Order 1003 became "permanent" peacetime legislation in 1948, largely because of this sustained militancy:

> The fall of 1945 marking the return to peace was hailed by both parties— not altogether secretly—as a testing time: was collective bargaining to dominate the field of labour relations or was it not? The showdown at Ford in Windsor in November-December and that at Stelco some months later were crucial.[7]

Thus the era of "free collective bargaining" came to be.

The use of the word "free" does have a crucial double meaning. It suggests that a balance of power prevails between capital and labour, that they face each other as equals, otherwise any bargain struck could scarcely be viewed as one which was "freely" achieved. It also suggests that the state's role is akin to one of umpire involved in applying, interpreting and adjusting impartial rules. In the first meaning, the structured inequality between capital and labour is obscured; in the second, the use of the state's coercive powers on behalf of capital falls from view. Industrial relations orthodoxy in the post-war era of free collective bargaining premised an acceptance of both meanings of the word "free." We will not dwell here on the continued structural inequality between capital and labour. It will suffice to mention the massive inequality in resources available to each party in the relationship. First, in sheer scale, flexibility and durability, capital's material resources continued to overwhelm those of labour. Second, the organizational and ideological resources of labour remained scarcely measurable against the network of associations, organizations, advisory bodies, in-house publications, and mass media, which were owned by, or financially beholden to, capital. Finally, capital's greater access to the state throughout the post-war period has been well documented.[8] The supremacy of capital in this era of free collective bargaining, in both its ideological and coercive dimensions, was captured well by Harold Laski:

> The right to call on the service of the armed forces ... is normally and naturally regarded as a proper prerogative of the ownership of some physical property that is seen to be in danger ... But we should be

overwhelmed if a great trade union in an industrial dispute, asked for, much less received, the aid of the police, or the militia or the federal troops to safeguard it in a claim to the right to work which it argued was as real as the physical right to visible and corporal property, like a factory.[9]

Laski, or course, recognized that in "a political democracy set within the categories of capitalist economies ... the area within which workers can manoeuvre for concessions is far wider than in a dictatorship." But he also understood the fact that even within capitalist democracy, the labour movement is confronted with "an upper limit to its efforts beyond which it is hardly likely to pass."[10]

This reference to capital's privileged access to the coercive apparatus of the state brings us directly to the second meaning of "free" within the term. For the limits beyond which labour was "hardly likely to pass" were not left to the imagination in Canadian labour policy after World War II. The very same legislation which supported the right to recognition and guaranteed the right to strike, also constrained the nature of bargaining and the exercise of union power in a highly detailed manner. The true thrust of the legislation in this respect, has been laid bare unwittingly by labour lawyer Paul Weiler, in defence of the conventional interpretation of "free" collective bargaining:

> There are two parts of a labour code which are central to the balance of power between union and employer. One is the use of the law to facilitate the growth of union representation of organized workers. The other is the use of the law to limit the exercise of union economic weapons (the strike and the picket line) once a collective bargaining relationship has become established.[11]

The "other" part of the labour legislation of the 1940s, to which Weiler referred, was precisely the extensive set of restrictions placed on collective action by unions, establishing one of the most restrictive and highly juridified frameworks for collective bargaining in any capitalist democracy. Modelled after the U.S. Wagner Act, Canadian legislation went "beyond it," as Logan noted: "(1) in naming and proscribing unfair practices by unions.... (2) in assuming a responsibility by the state to assist the two negotiating parties.... [and] (3) in forbidding strikes and lockouts during negotiations and for the term of the agreement."[12] Part and parcel of union recognition and the promotion of collective bargaining were a broad set of legal restrictions on eligibility for membership, and the precise circumstances for legal strike action. Apart from restrictions on picketing and secondary boycotts, the most important restriction on the right to strike— and the device ultimately used in 1982 to abrogate the right to strike in the public sector—was the ban on strikes during the term of a collective agreement.

It is critical to understand that the new mechanisms promoting the institutionalization of union recognition and free collective bargaining were, as Rand said, "devised to adjust, toward an increasing harmony, the interests of capital, labour and the public," in light of the shift in the balance of class forces that had taken place. It was an adjustment devised not to undermine but to secure and maintain under new conditions capital's "long run...dominant position."[13] The post-war settlement between capital and labour, involving limited measures to reduce unemployment and the introduction of welfare state reforms, as well as the new labour legislation, certainly entailed real gains for working people. These reforms, however, did not create equality between the contending classes. Rather, they fashioned a new hegemony for capital in Canadian society. Through formal mechanisms for negotiation and redistribution, consent came to play a visibly dominant role in inter-class relations, while coercion, still crucially present, was in the background. Coercion in capital-labour relations became less *ad hoc* and arbitrary: as the state's rationalization and institutionalization of workers' freedom of association became more formal, so did coercion. What before had taken the appearance of the Mountie's charge, now increasingly took the form of the rule of law by which unions policed themselves in most instances. Where they did not, the courts—with most of Canada's judges all too rarely following Rand in his sagacity or sense of social justice—were often quick to act with injunctions and additional restrictions on picketing that reflected a judicial perpetuation, alongside the new legal framework, of the tradition of *ad hoc* interventions to the benefit of capital.

Finally, even in the context of the overarching theme of consensual industrial relations that marked the era, it was still necessary to distinguish between what the state regarded as "legitimate" as opposed to "illegitimate" trade unionism. On political grounds even more blatant than those at the beginning of the century, the state and the bulk of the reformist wing of the labour leadership cooperated in applying extensive coercion, overtly as well as covertly, against communists and other radicals in the union movement. Many of labour's most committed and able industrial organizers, not only had their civil liberties abused, but also were pushed out of, or at least marginalized within, the trade unions—in the context of an international Cold War that often involved a very hot war against political radicalism in the domestic labour movement, and which lasted right through the 1950s. This too, was an element in the "post-war settlement," and an important measure of the state coercion—as well as of the unions' self-policing—embedded in it.

The Myth of Gradualism

The passage of the 1948 *Industrial Relations and Disputes Investigation Act* by the federal government, accompanied by similar provincial legislation, signified that legal protection of workers' freedom to organize and bargain would be, in fact, a central element of the post war "settlement." The labour movement undoubtedly expected that the reforms were "permanent" gains which would be gradually extended to other workers, and perhaps liberalized.[14] Moreover, given that the settlement also expanded the role of the state, substantial growth in the number of public sector workers was ensured. It might have been expected that the extension of bargaining rights would begin among public employees.[15] There was, however, little growth of bargaining rights in the post-war decades. In general, the unionized proportion of the non-agricultural workforce remained close to the 1948 figure of 30 per cent until the mid-1960s. Until that time, there was no extension of legislative protection in the fast growing public sector;

indeed, the only changes involved the imposition of additional restrictions on existing collective rights.[16]

The end to this impasse came, not gradually, but suddenly, in the mid-1960s. The decade of the sixties is frequently portrayed as one of student radicalism and militancy contrasted with working-class consumerism and acquiescence.[17] This contrast is much overdrawn as the "revolt" of the sixties was, in broad measure, a generational one. More importantly, consumerism is not without its contradictions. As Ralph Miliband observed in taking issue with the omnipotence ascribed to corporate demand management through advertising by John Galbraith and others: "The point is rather that business is able freely to propagate an ethos in which private acquisitiveness is made to appear as the main if not the only avenue to fulfillment, in which 'happiness' or 'success' are therefore defined in terms of private acquisition...."[18]

"Happiness" and "success" are, however, relative terms. By the 1960s, the character of the working class was being transformed as much by the post-war generation as were the universities. Young workers' frame of reference did not include the Depression or the Cold War; they had been raised when the myth of a classless, affluent society was incessantly propagated. The contrast between this image and the reality of working-class life did not so much tarnish the image as inspire them to make it part of their own reality.[19] Increasingly, the only way to achieve incomes consistent with the image was through collective bargaining, an understanding which was manifest in the mid-1960s wave of strikes as workers challenged the authority of their bosses and even the law under conditions of high employment. This wave began in the early 1960s, and at its peak in 1966, it established a new record in terms of the number of strikes and workers involved. As Stuart Jamieson noted, moreover, these strikes differed sharply from those of the 1950s in that wage demands figured much more prominently and an uncommonly large number of strikes—one-third of the total in 1966—were "wildcats," occasionally marked by violence, often conducted in defiance of union leaders and, at times, even against them. Workers' realization of their bargaining power and their determination to use it, not surprisingly, was seen by the government as a manifestation of an industrial relations crisis, prompting it to establish the famous Woods Task Force, the major post-war inquiry on labour relations.

The state's response to this new climate cannot be understood, however, except in relation to the particular, and even more profound, set of changes at work in Quebec.[20] In Quebec, the previous twenty-five years had seen a transformation of both the economic base and the working class, including the growth of unionization. Despite this transformation, the provincial state remained in the grip of conservative interests. The Quebec government's response to a succession of strikes, from the 1949 Asbestos Strike through to the strike by copper miners and smelter workers at Murdochville in 1957, was hostile and repressive, fostering a relatively radical working class and intelligentsia. The 1961 election victory of the Lesage Liberals formally broke the hold of the "ancien regime" on the Quebec state, and initiated belated and rapid political change in the province. This change necessitated a political settlement with labour no less than that which had been necessary elsewhere in Canada in the 1940s. The basis of this

TABLE II
Strikes and Lockouts in Canada 1960-75

	Number	Workers involved	Work-days duration	% of estimated working time
1960	274	49,408	738,700	.06
1961	287	97,959	1,335,080	.11
1962	311	74,332	1,417,900	.11
1963	332	83,428	917,140	.07
1964	343	100,535	1,580,550	.11
1965	501	171,870	2,349,870	.17
1966	617	411,459	5,178,170	.34
1967	522	252,018	3,974,760	.25
1968	582	223,562	5,082,732	.32
1969	595	306,799	7,751,880	.46
1970	542	261,706	6,539,560	.39
1971	569	239,631	2,866,590	.16
1972	598	706,474	7,753,530	.43
1973	724	348,470	5,776,080	.30
1974	1218	580,912	9,221,890	.46
1975	1171	506,443	10,908,810	.53

SOURCE: Canada, Department of Labour, Strikes and Lockouts in Canada (1975), Table 1, p. 6

settlement was the extension of bargaining rights to Quebec's public sector workers in 1965. The breakthrough in Quebec sent shockwaves reverberating through the Canadian state because the reforms went well beyond what had been achieved in English Canada. In Quebec, federal public sector workers were part of the politicization process of the working class and were galvanized to intensify their efforts to win the same demands from their own employer. Pressure from Quebec was a powerful boost to the growing insistence of federal workers generally for bargaining rights after the Diefenbaker government, faced with the 1958-61 recession, broke precedent by rejecting the pay increase proposed by the bi-partite National Joint Council which, since 1944, advised the government on these matters.[21]

It was clear that significant political restructuring was inevitable, not only in Quebec but also at the federal level. The Quebec Liberal party, reflecting the initiatives of the radical petit bourgeois intelligentsia, provided a beacon to the Federal Liberals who needed to find a new image after the St. Laurent-C.D. Howe Government of the 1950s was routed by the populist Diefenbaker Conservatives in 1958. The apparent appeal of the recently formed New Democratic Party (NDP) and the fading bloom of post-war settlement across English Canada, intensified the Liberal Party's need for a new image, which they hoped would bring them a quick return to their accustomed position as the "governing" party. At the federal level, the new reality was reflected in the rise of the "three wise men," Trudeau,

Pelletier and Marchand, to the leadership of the Liberal Party. The "second wave" of the welfare state in Canada, undertaken by the minority Liberal governments of the mid-1960s, was in good part an outcome of these developments. A significant element of this, apart from medicare and pension reforms, was the appointment of the Heeney Commission in 1963 to examine the question of collective bargaining rights for federal workers. It was a foregone conclusion that Heeney would recommend in favour of collective bargaining for federal workers; what was at issue was how "free" it really would be.

The government's commitment to the rights of its workers was no deeper than that of capital. As employers, governments have a unique rationale for restricting their employees' freedom of association—the supremacy of parliament. As a result, while finally conceding federal employees' collective bargaining rights in 1967, the federal government insisted on restrictions beyond those imposed on private sector workers. Vital issues, including pensions, job classifications, technological change, staffing, and use of part-time or casual labour, were wholly or partly excluded from the scope of bargaining. Serious consideration was given to denying federal workers the right to strike as well, but in the end, the right to strike was granted, largely because the postal employees, particularly in Quebec and British Columbia, waged a number of what, in effect, were recognition strikes in the mid-1960s. These strikes did much to persuade the government that making strikes illegal did not guarantee preventing them.[22]

The reverberations of the "Quiet Revolution" in Quebec were also felt in the other provinces, where collective bargaining became the order of the day for most public sector workers. While the meaningfulness of these reforms is beyond doubt, nonetheless, it is striking how restricted a version of trade union freedoms was conceded. The challenge to the law which the 1960s wave of strikes often represented, was met, not by liberalizing, but by broadening the inclusiveness of Canada's restrictive, legalized, collective bargaining regime. In most provinces, and at the federal level, a number of crucial issues were decreed to be outside the scope of public sector bargaining. In several cases—i.e. Alberta, Ontario, Prince Edward Island and Nova Scotia—provincial employees, and often, others such as hospital workers, were still denied the right to strike.[23]

The Limits of Reform

The much touted "breakthrough," extending union rights in Canada in the 1960s, must therefore be seen in terms of their continually narrowing limits. It would be wrong to ascribe these limits just to the resistance of particular sections of capital or to the ideology of liberal politicians. An equally important and largely ignored factor was the remarkable conservatism of the English Canadian labour movement, which repeatedly proved itself incapable of taking the initiative in generating demands or mobilizing support for reforms challenging the terms of the post-war settlement. Few Canadian trade union leaders, for example, questioned the principle of the ban on strikes during the life of a collective agreement, although they sometimes sought specific exemptions from its application (e.g. unsafe working conditions, technological change). They even went along with the requirement that they act as agents of the law by formally notifying their members of the legal obligation to abide by this ban. During the 1960s and early 1970s, union leaders occasionally joined their members in defying the law as it applied to a given dispute, but they very rarely questioned the general framework of legal regulation.

This conservatism must be attributed in part to the effects of the Cold War on the labour movement, as already noted. The anti-communist crusade after World War II was directed against socialist ideas and militant rank-and-file struggle, as much as at members of the Communist Party who then symbolized, albeit imperfectly and not exclusively, that tradition. As a result, control of the labour movement was assumed by people who were characterized, as David Lewis delicately put it, "by the absence of a sense of idealism."[24] There is, of course, no little irony in Lewis' providing this description, given that his own central role in trying to build a base for the CCF in the union movement involved him in trying "to wrest control from the communists wherever possible."[25] In this struggle, the CCF allied with the most conservative and opportunistic elements of the union leadership, who, upon winning this internecine struggle, placed their own indelible stamp on the labour movement.

But other factors were involved as well, not least because objective circumstances typically exert more influence over action than subjective intention. In this respect, the adverse effect of the 1940s legislation on the character of the Canadian labour movement must enter into our consideration. Bourgeois reforms, however much they are the product of class struggle, are not without their contradictions. Left unchallenged they can undermine the very conditions which called them into existence, opening the way for future defeats. In reflecting on the approach to union recognition of the legislation, H.A. Logan observed that, "The powerful weapon of the strike as an aid to negotiation through militant organisation, was weakened in its usefulness where the approach to recognition had to be certification."[26] Logan's reference to the way the legislation devalued militant organization is of crucial importance. Unlike the capitalist firm, with its naturally given singularity of purpose, unions aggregate discrete individuals with their own purposes. The power of unions lies in the willingness of their numbers to *act* collectively, and for that to happen, a common purpose must be *developed*.[27] This is, of course, a social process—an outcome of education and organization involving sustained interaction between leaders and the led—and one requiring particular skills. Moreover, the incessant centrifugal pressures of a liberal consumerist society make this a never-ending process.

The certification approach to recognition did more than just weaken the apparent importance of militant organization. It directed the efforts of union leaders away from mobilizing and organizing and toward the juridical arena of the labour boards. In this context, different skills were necessary. It was crucial, above all, to know the "law"—including legal rights, procedures, and precedents. These activities tended to foster a legalistic practice and consciousness in which union rights appeared as privileges bestowed by the state, rather than democratic freedoms won, and to be defended by, collective struggle.[28] The ban on strikes during collective agreements and the institution of compulsory arbitration to resolve disputes while agreements were in force had a similar effect. Under these circumstances, it was unnecessary to maintain and develop collective organization between negotiations. Indeed, union leaders had a powerful incentive to do the reverse: to suppress any sign of spontaneous militancy. Industrial relations legislation inevitably treats unions as legal entities which are distinct from their members. This was evidenced by the much greater penalties for union officials who violate the law compared to those for members. This intensified the pressure on union officials to act as agents of social control over their members, rather than their spokespersons and organizers.

The corrosive effects on union democracy of this kind of juridical and ideological structuring are severe.[29] The trade unionism which developed in Canada during the post-war years, bore all the signs of the web of legal restrictions which enveloped it. Its practice and consciousness were highly legalistic and bureaucratic, and therefore, its collective strength limited. These characteristics were reflected in the acceptance of the greater restrictions on public employees' freedom of association by the broader labour movement. Moreover, the existing labour movement provided no other inspiration or example than legalism for public sector unions. This model was particularly debilitating for those public sector unions which had engaged in little of the mobilization and struggle for recognition which was so much a part of the formation of the original labour movement, and which had characterized the industrial unions in the period prior to the post-war settlement. Thus, a union like the Public Service Alliance of Canada in contrast to the Canadian Union of Postal Workers, (CUPW), was one borne almost entirely of legalism, rather than mobilization and struggle.

This, of course, is not to suggest that all the newly recognized public sector unions were content with what had been offered them. For many, the limited rights acquired were seen as a way station on the road to obtain trade union rights equivalent to those enjoyed in the private sector. As events unfolded, however, this proved to be a naively optimistic view. By the time that the way station had been reached, in the late 1960s, the roadbed was already crumbling. The state had to contend with the wage pressure of organized workers while adjusting to the constraints placed upon it by the emerging crisis of capitalism.

CHAPTER 3

The Turn to Coercion: Permanent Exceptionalism

In the present state of society, in fact, it is the *possibility* of the strike which enables workers to negotiate with their employers on terms of approximate equality. It is wrong to think that the unions are in themselves able to secure this equality. If the right to strike is suppressed, or seriously limited, the trade union movement becomes nothing more than one institution among many in the service of capitalism: a convenient organization for disciplining the workers, occupying their leisure time, and ensuring their profitability for business

Pierre Elliot Trudeau (1956)[1]

The wave of industrial militancy which arose in the mid-1960s, continued on into the early seventies. Instead of abating, it reached a new crest with the newly unionized public sector workers often taking the lead.[2] The heightened degree of industrial conflict, however, reflected both greater militancy on the part of workers, and more determined resistance by capital and the state, in light of the deepening economic crisis. The long post-war boom led many to believe that economic growth was unproblematic; that, if capitalism had not quietly passed away, its anarchic character had been subdued by governments armed with Keynesian theory.[3] But this boom could not, and did not, last. The seventies have been characterized by "stagflation;" growth rates below the level necessary for full employment, combined with severe inflationary tendencies. In such conditions, the margin for concessions to secure labour's consent no longer existed; indeed, capital increasingly required concessions. Faced with stagnant or shrinking markets, rising resource prices, increased foreign competition, and a labour movement ready to defend its living standards, capital experienced reduced profit margins on existing investments and few profitable new opportunities.

One response to this situation by governments, both in Canada and elsewhere, involved new subsidies to capital in the form of loans, grants, and tax concessions, thus underwriting investment and shifting the cost of the welfare state onto employed workers.[4] But these initiatives had little impact on growth and tended to exacerbate inflation since organized workers responded militantly to preserve their real incomes. Government deficits ballooned as expenditures rose on corporate subsidies, the unemployed, and public sector wages. The other major response by the state was to restrict the bargaining power of organized labour. Governments tried one way by obtaining the "voluntary" agreement of union leaders to limit members' wage demands to some agreed level, in exchange for a union role in state economic decision-making and a promise of reforms enhancing union security, marginal extensions of the welfare state, or both.[5] The governments' other strategy was to deploy the state's coercive powers against the labour movement with increasing vigor. *These two strategies should not be seen as mutually exclusive.* Coercive measures, intentionally or otherwise, prompted unions to rethink their opposition to "voluntary" restraint. On the other hand, the inability of the state to deliver a *quid pro quo* in a form of the "social wage," because of the growing economic crisis, undermined the viability of the voluntary restraint option and forced the state to adopt more coercive measures.

Initially, government policy at the federal and provincial levels reflected both strategies. In 1969/70, and again in 1974/75, the federal government held discussions with the Canadian Labour Congress (CLC) aimed at securing voluntary wage restraint.[6] In a number of jurisdictions, there were reforms enhancing union security and workers' collective rights. Among these were a relaxation of the restrictions on secondary picketing in British Columbia; expansion of the rights to refuse unsafe work in Ontario and Saskatchewan and at the federal level; provisions for imposing "first agreements" on recalcitrant employers in British Columbia, Ontario and Quebec; and most significantly, extensive limitations on the use of strike breakers by the P.Q. government elected in 1976 in Quebec. Nonetheless, as the decade of the 1970s wore on, the shift toward new coercive measures was particularly striking.

This shift was above all reflected in the rising incidence of *ad hoc* back-to-work legislation at both the federal and provincial levels. In the first fifteen years after 1950, there were only six instances of back-to-work legislation in total; there were *fifty-one* such instances in the following decade-and-a-half, with half of these from 1975-79 alone. Yet another forty-three such measures were to follow in the 1980-87 period.

The first post-war instance of such legislation in 1950, was used by the federal government against the railway workers, striking for a forty-hour week and a pay increase. The justification then for the legislation, as later, to quote Prime Minister St. Laurent, was that "the welfare and security of the nation are imperiled."[7] Not surprisingly, St. Laurent insisted that it was "not designed to establish precedents or procedures for subsequent bargaining negotiations."[8] Events were to prove otherwise as railway workers were threatened with similar legislation in 1954, and actually subjected to it again in 1960 and 1966. The

TABLE III
Back-To-Work Measures 1950-1987[9]

	Federal	Provincial	Total	Annual Averages
1950-54	1	0	1	.2
1955-59	1	1	2	.4
1960-64	2	1	3	.6
1965-69	2	8	10	2.0
1970-74	4	12	16	3.4
1975-79	6	19	25	5.0
1980-84	1	21	22	4.4
1985-87	3	18	21	7.0
Total		20	80	100.0

increased frequency and wider application of back-to-work legislation that followed were not the only notable trends in the state's use of this weapon. Over time, governments have, after the onset of a dispute, introduced such legislation with greater dispatch and less parliamentary debate, including increasingly onerous penalties for defiance of the law.

This new reliance on back-to-work legislation was part of a broader pattern of developments, one which characterized the onset of a new era in state policy toward labour. What marked this transformation was a shift from the generalized rule-of-law form of coercion (whereby an overall legal framework both establishes and constrains the rights and powers of all unions), toward a form of selective, *ad hoc*, discretionary state coercion (whereby the state removes for a specific purpose and period the rights contained in labour legislation). We began to witness a return to the pre-World War II era of "*ad hoc* suspension of hostilities." This time, however, the *ad hoc* policy was not designed to avoid or delay the *establishment* of freedom of association; rather it sought to contain or repress manifestations of class conflict as practised *within* the institutionalized freedom of association. Actions legal under general legislation increasingly were declared unlawful for particular groups of workers, or for all workers, for a particular period of time. When it becomes common to resort to rhetoric and emergency powers to override the general framework of freedoms, there is clearly a crisis in the old form of rule.

The treatment accorded to cupw by the federal government, in 1978, illustrates this crisis. At that time, the government publicly stated *in advance of a strike* that it would not tolerate the union's exercise of its legal right to strike. Once the strike began, the government immediately invoked back-to-work legislation, the *Postal Services Continuation Act*, Bill C-8, which revived the previous collective agreement and overrode the relatively small penalties in the *Public Service Staff Relations Act*, to establish potentially unlimited penalties. Finally, the government charged the union's leader, J.C. Parrot, not for encouraging his members to defy the back-to-work law, but for *remaining silent*; that is for not publicly urging them to obey the law.[10] Similar requirements for union leaders, specified in previous back-to-work legislation, had escaped notice because they were either obeyed, or if not, were disregarded by the government. In charging Mr. Parrot, and in granting him bail only on the condition that he tell cupw members what the law required, the state set aside not only the general legal provisions for the union's right to strike but also the protection of free speech contained in the *Bill of Rights*.

The use of back-to-work legislation primarily concerned public sector workers. The statutory incomes policy of the Anti-Inflation Programme of 1975-78, suspended free collective bargaining for *all* workers. It was initiated by the government and upheld by the courts on the basis of an elastic definition of economic emergency. Once again, the rules of the game established in the post-war settlement were set aside through special legislation. This empowered the Anti-Inflation Board to examine newly negotiated agreements and roll back wage increases exceeding the government's guidelines. The Act created an "Administrator" to enforce a Board report or Cabinet order, backed by onerous penalties of unlimited fines and five years imprisonment. The new spirit of the era was adequately expressed by Prime Minister Trudeau when he cynically told a radio interviewer immediately after the initiation of the Anti-Inflation Programme, "We'll put a few union leaders in jail for three years and others will get the message."[11]

It is now virtually, universally conceded that despite the government's rhetoric about equivalent wage, price, dividend and profit restraint under the Anti-Inflation Programme, the substantive aspect of the policy entailed only wage controls. Primer Minister Trudeau, in his October 1982 cbc broadcasts referred to a comprehensive but temporary statutory prices and incomes policy of the type in force from 1975-78 as follows: "... what controls are for is to place the coercive use of government power between Canadians, like a referee who pushes boxers apart and forces them to their corners to rest up so that they can hit each other again."[12] A more appropriate metaphor for the 1975-78 case would have the referee holding the arms of one of the boxers while the other flailed away.

A New Ideology For The 1980s

The 1975 wage controls coincided with the inauguration of monetarism as the guiding practice of monetary policy in Canada, while fiscal policy in the last years of the 1970s showed a growing tendency toward "belt-tightening." Although defeated in the 1979 election (a common fate for Western governments which have introduced statutory wage controls), the Trudeau Liberals swept back to office nine months later as suddenly "born again" reformers, clothing themselves with all the themes first raised in the late 1960s: a patriated Constitution; enhanced civil liberties; income redistribution through tax reform; and a programme of economic nationalism. The new government was able to make good on the first two themes through the *Constitution Act 1982*, including the new *Charter of Rights and Freedoms*. But the 1981 reform budget was aborted (just as the Carter Royal Commission proposals had been in the late 1960s) in the face of vociferous capitalist opposition, backed by threats of a capital strike. And although the ambitious National Energy Programme was introduced and kept in place until it was undone by the Mulroney Government, the furor it aroused from Washington to Edmonton ensured it was not only the first but also the last effective shot across the bow of continentalism. In all of this, the impact of the sharp 1981-82 recession played a crucial contributory role. Striving to prove their respectability in the face of the crisis, the Liberals found themselves engulfed. As inflation and unemployment levels reached unprecedented post-war highs, and as business confidence fell to corresponding lows, the last Trudeau Government turned from a policy of enhancing civil liberties and controls on American capital, to legal controls on Canadian workers which severely restricted their liberties. In so doing, a critical new phase in the turn to coercion was inaugurated.

Clearly, the federal government's 1982 "6 and 5" programme was not a "bolt out of the blue"—an isolated blemish on an otherwise impeccable record of liberal reformism. But its significance lay in the fact that it served as the opening shot in a broad-based assault on trade union freedoms by federal and provincial governments in the 1980s. It made explicit the *ad hoc*, selective, "temporary" use of coercion, not merely directed at the particular groups of workers affected or at the particular issue of "emergency" at hand, but rather designed to set an example for what was considered to be appropriate behaviour throughout the industrial relations system.[13] The suspension, in 1982, of public sector workers' rights was not proclaimed or defended in terms of what it would directly accomplish to stem inflation and re-invigorate Canadian capitalism; rather, it was an example of what other workers had to voluntarily do if these objectives were to be attained.

What characterized the new policy was not only the unprecedented severity of *ad hoc* coercive measures by the state, but also the construction of a new ideology generalizing the state's new coercive role to the working class as a whole. Because this new ideology was not legally codified in the manner of the post-war settlement, because it did not *universally* remove the right to strike and the right to "free collective bargaining," the new state coercion was, paradoxically, capable of being ideologically portrayed as "voluntary." Thus, the Prime Minister's October 1982 broadcasts to the nation emphatically declared that the government had explicitly rejected the option of the "coercive use of government power":

> Controls could not create the trust in each other and belief in our country that alone would serve our future. Controls would declare, with the force of the law, that Canadians cannot trust Canadians.... To choose to fight inflation, as a free people acting together—that is the course we chose.[14]

The presentation of increased state coercion in this confusing way was conditional upon three elements. The first was a form of ideological excommunication regarding the rights of public sector workers as Canadian citizens. The draconian controls established over them in 1982, were hidden amidst careful phrases asserting that only *"comprehensive controls"* were coercive and contrary to the principle of a "free people acting together." The controls were rather "examples" for other workers' "voluntarism." That this sleight of hand could even be attempted rested upon the fact that, for a decade, state employees had been presented as parasites, and state services, not long ago understood as essential to the community and social justice, were denigrated as wasteful and unproductive.

The second element necessary to this "voluntarist" depiction of coercion was that the specific coercive acts, such as back-to-work legislation, designation and statutory incomes policies, had to be continually portrayed as exceptional, temporary, or emergency-related; regardless of how frequently they occurred, regardless of the number of workers who fell within their scope or were threatened by their "example." Since the terminology of emergency and crisis can be made elastic enough to cover a whole era rather than just specific events, months, or even years, measures presented as temporary can characterize an entire historical period.

Finally, and perhaps most importantly, the voluntary ideological veneer rested upon the construction of a new set of norms to justify labour's subordinate role within capitalism. The post-war settlement sought to maintain the dominant position of capital by establishing legal rights for organized labour to protect the workers' immediate material interests in a capitalist system. The ideology of the new era reversed this earlier logic. It placed the onus on labour to maintain capitalism as a viable economic system by acquiescing to capital's demand for the restriction or suspension of workers' previously recognized rights and freedoms, as well as sacrificing their immediate material interests. Whereas the "question of social justice" was key to the construction of the hegemony of the 1940s, Trudeau's appeal to "trust and belief" became the key phrase in the effort to reconstitute it in the 1980s.

It must be stressed that Trudeau and his government did not stand alone in effecting the construction of the "trust and belief" element of the new ideology. They were aided, implicitly at least, by a bevy of industrial relations experts, many of whom are recognized publicly for their "pro-labour" sentiments. A good example was provided by Paul Weiler's highly influential book *Reconcilable Differences: New Directions in Labour Law*. At one level, his book, published in 1980, displayed with refreshing candour the dilemmas of liberal reformism in its attempt to combine a spirited defence of the right to strike with a model of state intervention ensuring that this right would not be disruptive to capital. At another level, it was an unwitting contribution to the construction of the new ideology in that it attempted to justify statutory incomes policies as being in labour's interests. Weiler acknowledged that the 1975-78 Anti-Inflation Programme only involved effective wage restraint, adding that for economic (the "openness" of Canada's economy) and political (capitalist objections, the evils of bureaucracy) reasons, such programmes cannot do more than restrain incomes. Nor did he view wage increases as the sole cause of inflation. Nonetheless, he commended controls (if not the government's lack of candour) to labour, arguing that it was in labour's interests to acquiesce to such policies. The uncertainty that inflation creates "interferes with rational business planning and investment," thereby reducing the rate of job creation; and, by making Canadian products less competitive internationally, it threatens "unemployment in our plants and factories." Controls in this context "*facilitate* an orderly winding down of inflation...with a minimum of disruption and unemployment."[15] In other words, labour should eschew efforts to defend its economic interests directly and instead entrust its future to capital. It was also *this logic*, strongly contrasting as it was with Bill Bennett's and Peter Lougheed's neo-conservative, anti-union logic, which played a role in implicitly promoting "temporary" coercive state interventions in the 1980s.

The Federal Government Leads....

The coercive assault of 1982-84 comprised three movements: first, the generalization of the federal government's "6 and 5" restraint legislation, temporarily removing the right to strike from most public sector workers in Canada; second, the partial extension of the restraints to the private sector; and thirdly, the increasing frequency of permanent legislation restricting trade union rights.[16]

The *Public Sector Compensation Restraint Act* (Bill C-124), introduced in June 1982, was not as comprehensive as the *Anti-Inflation Act* of 1975-78 which covered both public and private sector workers. However, what it lacked in comprehensiveness, it more than made up in the severity of treatment of the workers it covered. Bill C-124 abrogated the right to strike and bargain collectively by extending existing collective agreements for two years. Since strikes during agreements were prohibited under the earlier legislation, the new Act cynically used the same legislation which had established it to deny free collective bargaining for two to three years. This denial went so far as to "roll back" signed agreements with increases above the 6 and 5 per cent annual limits during the life of the Act. The Act also gave sweeping powers to the Treasury Board to enforce compliance and designate affected employees.

Ottawa's "6 and 5" programme suspended collective bargaining and extended *all of the terms* of the existing agreements, unilaterally. All wage increases were to be determined by the government and awarded to public sector employees *without* negotiation. For employees earning over $49,000, no merit increment or performance payments were allowed. Significantly, the largest rollback of a negotiated contract—from 12.25 per cent to 6 per cent—affected the lowest paid employees in the federal government, the largely female clerical and regulatory groups earning an average of $18,000.

The government began phasing out the "6 and 5" programme on June 30, 1984, with the exit period for some employees lasting till December 1985. The Lalonde Budget of February 15, 1984, announced that the government would persist in public sector wage restraint, with no catch-up payments compensating for losses during the controls period. In addition, all settlements had to be based on total package comparisons with, and not exceeding, the private sector. Settlements should continue contributing to lower inflation. Finally, any return to free collective bargaining was qualified by Lalonde's declaration of his intention to amend the *Public Service Staff Relations Act* and impose wage changes through legislation if "...reasonable wage settlements cannot be obtained...."

The "6 and 5" programme was never intended to affect federal public sector workers alone. Not only were the provinces expected to, and largely did, subject their employees to similar measures, but capital was also to be "inspired." This inspiration was primarily pursued at the ideological level, as we have noted; however, the Trudeau government also offered a more "practical" lead in the summer of 1983. After a settlement in the Nova Scotia construction industry that summer, which exceeded the "6 and 5" ceilings, Finance Minister Marc Lalonde, responding to business fears of a construction-led union wage spiral, reacted swiftly. The Minister requested an immediate meeting of Canadian Construction Association (CCA) officials to discuss measures to prevent "excessive" settlements, with the CCA in turn calling for Lalonde to meet with all provincial Finance and Labour Ministers "to examine the grossly unfair monopoly unions hold over employers in the unionized sector of the industry."[17] The contractors' association clearly saw this as an opportunity to push their opposition to the *Federal Fair Wages and Hours of Work Act*. This Act had been enacted in 1938 to prevent unscrupulous contractors from winning bids on federally-financed construction projects at the expense of unorganized, low-paid and overworked tradesmen. Over the 1970s, the CCA had taken a firm position against rigid enforcement of the Act, because of increasing competition in the private sector from non-unionized firms, pressing it upon successive federal Ministers of Labour. Lalonde called a meeting with provincial Finance Ministers to discuss a coordinated approach on July 27, 1983. He sent a letter to his provincial counterparts announcing that the Act would be suspended in those provinces where wage settlements in the construction industry exceeded "6 and 5," beginning with Nova Scotia and Ontario, and applying through 1983-84. This action, subsequently applied to Prince Edward Island and lifted only in Ontario in August 1984 during the federal election campaign, was the prelude, perhaps even the signal, to the anti-union stances taken by the British Columbia and Alberta governments in the construction industry. The disputes over this action predominated the labour scene in those provinces in 1984.

Even more significant was the novel use of designations to remove the right to strike from public sector workers. Under the 1967 legislation extending collective bargaining to federal public employees, the government had reserved the right to designate certain jobs as "essential for the safety and security of the public" and hence to deny the workers performing these jobs the right to strike. The Public Service Staff Relations Board defined "safety and security" rather narrowly, so that the right to strike could not be vitiated by the indiscriminate use of designations,[18] and the government had accepted the Board's definition. This practice was shattered in 1982, when the government, intent on designating away the right to strike of virtually the whole air traffic controllers' group, successfully challenged the Board's definition of "safety and security" in the Supreme Court[19] As a result, the government was free to designate anyone whose normal work activities, *in the government's own view*, affected the safety and security of the public.

The meaning of the government's new-found freedom to define the bargaining rights of its workforce is graphically revealed in Table IV, which looks at the change in the use of designations by the Treasury Board. The Table is based upon all bargaining groups which resumed negotiations in 1984 (in the wake of the "6 and 5" programme) and compares the number of positions they proposed to designate in that year with the number they had proposed in the group's last set of negotiations, prior to the Supreme Court ruling.

TABLE IV
Treasury Board's Designation Proposals[20]

Bargaining Group	1984 Proposal Number	1984 Proposal % of Group	Preceding Proposal Number	Preceding Proposal % of Group
Engineering & Scientific Support	2,438	33	1,028	14
Data Processors	2,078	63	758	25
Communications	601	79	347	44
Clerks	18,041	36	9,575	20
Corrections Staff	5,128	100	4,918	100
General Labour & Trades	11,580	68	4,071	21
General Services, Cleaners	9,349	81	3,863	31
Heat & Power Workers	2,297	100	1,590	65
Hospital Staff	1,740	100	1,261	54
Ships Crews	2,654	100	1,764	65
Total/Average	55,906 / 75.9		29,175 / 46.9	

Prior to the Supreme Court ruling the Treasury Board proposed on average to designate 46 per cent of each bargaining unit, and in five cases (half of the total) designations were below one-third of the bargaining unit. In 1984, designations were averaging 75.9 per cent of each bargaining unit, and in every case at least one-third of the bargaining unit was designated.

In interpreting these figures it should be borne in mind that they, if anything, underestimated the real effects of the ruling. Prior to 1982 the Treasury Board's proposals were subject to the approval of the PSSRB which frequently lowered the number, whereas the proposals in 1984 were beyond the Board's purview. In any event, it is indisputable that the 1984 level of designations was sufficiently high to empty federal government workers' right to strike of a great deal of substance.

...The Provinces Follow—And How!

While "6 and 5" provided a lead for the provinces, their responses varied in significant respects. Ontario and Nova Scotia basically followed the federal model. Ontario's *Inflation Restraint Act* (Bill 179) unilaterally extended existing collective agreements for one year, with a 5 per cent maximum on compensation package increases effective September 21, 1982. Some agreements, for groups caught in a two-year control net, were subject to a transition year, with increases limited to a maximum of 9 per cent. The Ontario legislation covered 565,000 provincial, municipal and regional public servants and, additionally, employees of schools, hospitals, Crown corporations, boards and privately-owned, para-public sector companies contracted to, or funded by, the province, including day care, nursing homes and ambulance services. The Restraint Board established by the Act was given substantial powers to investigate, advise and issue binding orders restraining public sector compensation increases. Less noted than Bill 179, but also during this period, were the equally arbitrary rollbacks of negotiated increases to 5 per cent, imposed on Ontario Hydro workers and sixteen thousand City of Toronto manual and clerical workers in the Canadian Union of Public Employees.

Following the expiry of this restraint legislation, the Ontario government passed Bill 111, *Public Sector Prices and Compensation Review Act*, on December 13, 1983, which effectively maintained many of the restraints imposed earlier under Bill 179 for an additional one-year period. While returning to the form of free collective bargaining and normal dispute resolution mechanisms, the government's objective was to limit compensation increases to 5 per cent for the 600,000 employees covered by the Act, by restricting the wage component of public funding. Agreements had to be reported to and monitored by the Restraint Board, and the Bill also required arbitrators to take into account the employer's "ability to pay in light of existing fiscal policy" when handing down awards. The announced 5 per cent compensation criteria was only a guideline and the Board had no power to roll back settlements that exceeded the guide. However, the Board was empowered to recommend to the Treasurer that appropriate measures be taken to ensure conformity. Indeed, the Treasurer was extremely active in demanding such conformity throughout the public sector in 1984.

In Nova Scotia, the actual wage restraint programme came in two parts. In the initial phase, introduced shortly after the Ottawa programme of 1982, the province introduced guidelines of 6 per cent, compulsory for non-unionized employees and the basis for salary negotiations for unionized public employees; teachers, hospital, municipal, plus some Crown agency and board employees as well as provincial employees. At the same time, Premier Buchanan threatened compulsory legislation suspending collective bargaining if the unions did not comply. While collective agreements signed prior to September 15, 1982 would be honoured till expiration, any new agreements had to be concluded by February 28, 1983 or the government would *unilaterally impose* a settlement. The government postponed this deadline in early 1983, in hopes of voluntary union restraint. This failed, however, and the government enacted Bill 71, *An Act Respecting Compensation in the Public Sector*, on June 1, 1983. The twenty thousand public sector workers who had still not settled were forced to continue under the wage restraint legislation and the terms of the previous collective agreement, which, in effect, rolled back any non-monetary benefits they might have negotiated up to that point. For these and twenty-five thousand other provincial employees covered by the Act, the legislation imposed a 6 per cent *limit* during a one-year control period, staggered to coincide with the expiry of existing agreements. The Nova Scotia legislation also contained two features found in other restraint programmes. First, the Act was administered by a three-person board holding broad powers, with no appeal against any ruling. Second, union acceptance of the programmes in no way prevented the government from laying off employees.

Of the other Atlantic provinces, Prince Edward Island enacted the *Compensation Review Act* (Bill 39), in June 1983. It restricted total compensation increases over two years, beginning April 1, 1983, to a *maximum* of 5 per cent of the prior period's straight-time average hourly rate. Not more than 40 per cent of the increase could be in the first year. In addition, all settlements had to be submitted to a Compensation Review Commissioner, and meet certain criteria such as the precedent established by past settlements, employer's ability to pay, consideration of unemployment levels and impact on inflation. The Commissioner was empowered to assess whether a settlement was "fair and reasonable" and either to approve or reject it and appoint a mediator, or impose a settlement by rejecting the recommendations of the mediator. Thus, Bill 39 maintained a facade of "free collective bargaining;" but, through the sweeping powers of the Commissioner, it could arbitrarily impose settlements or break negotiated ones. New Brunswick and Newfoundland limited themselves to guidelines following "6 and 5," but in the case of Premier Peckford's government, the initial two-year programme was followed, in 1984, by a two-year wage freeze for provincial employees, including employees of Crown corporations and provincial institutions.

Quebec, ostensibly, did not follow the federal government's initiative, but the parallel actions of the P.Q. government still spoke of the essential unity of the Canadian state. In April 1982, the P.Q. asked public sector employees to forego the impending salary increases in their existing agreements due to expire in December 1982. As was their right under collective bargaining law, Quebec's Common Front public sector employees in the Quebec Teachers' Federation (CEQ), the Confederation of National Trade Unions (CSN) and the Quebec Federation of Labour (FTQ) offered to open up the entire collective agreement. The government refused, and in June 1982, legislated Bill 70, *An Act Respecting, Remuneration in the Public Sector*, which decreed, in advance of the expiry date, pay reductions averaging 19.5 per cent for 300,000 provincial public servants from January 1, 1983 to March 31, 1983. In effect, the government had removed the right to strike and extended collective agreements at lower salary levels. The Bill stated that, in other respects, the conditions of employment be maintained until new collective agreements were made.

Even this provision was repealed by the subsequent introduction of Bill 105, *An Act Respecting the Conditions of Employment in the Public Sector*, which unilaterally decreed collective agreements for public sector workers for three years, until December 1985. The Bill not only covered the same provincial employees as Bill 70, but also included previously exempt groups of public employees and employees of Montreal Transit. Its restraint package kept annual increases equal to the Consumer Price Index (CPI) minus 1.5 per cent. Hourly employees received increases equal to the CPI with many affected workers earning less at the end of 1985 than in 1982.

But, Bill 105 represented *even more* than restraint and abrogation of collective agreement processes. The Bill's accompanying 109 decrees, covering eighty thousand pages of text, significantly rewrote collective agreement terms regarding job security and working conditions. For example, in the severely hit education sector, there were cutbacks in staff, increases in workloads, increased administrative control over teacher distribution, changes in seniority clauses and ability to obtain "permanent" status, and extension of administration control over departmental policy.

Since Bill 105 effectively removed the right to strike until 1985, such severe legislation was bound to produce a reaction, given the P.Q.'s negotiating intransigence. The illegal walkout of Common Front public sector employees in late January 1983, led to even more draconian back-to-work legislation, strongly confirming the complete lack of respect for bargaining rights. In passing Bill 111 in February 1983, *An Act to Ensure the Resumption of Services in the Public Sector*, the P.Q. government provided fines, imprisonment, and decertification of bargaining agents if the strike did not end immediately. The Bill exempted Quebec from the *Canadian Charter of Rights and Freedoms* and suspended sections of the *Quebec Charter of Human Rights*. Absence from work by covered employees was considered *prima facie* evidence of guilt. Fines and firing could take place via a simple government order. Normal legal protection such as individual trials and the right to present evidence in one's defence were also removed. It even suspended normal hiring procedures. Opposed by the Bar Association, civil liberties and human rights groups, Bill 111 represented an unprecedented attack on trade union rights and civil liberties.

Permanent Restrictions

The much-vaunted Western Canadian alienation from the Trudeau government didn't extend to its anti-union legislation. This was most clearly seen in the support those provincial governments gave to the highly centralist Anti-Inflation Programme from 1975-78. Reciprocally, it could be said the British Columbia government's wage restraint programme, introduced at the beginning of 1982, inspired the national wave of "temporary" controls later that year. Ominously, after the re-election of the Bennett government in the spring of 1983, temporary restraint in the public sector was extended to sweeping *permanent* restrictions in the whole framework of labour legislation, representing the most sustained assault on trade union rights in Canada. As we shall see, this extension was confined neither to British Columbia, nor to the West for that matter.

In February 1982, with industrial settlements averaging 15 per cent, the B.C. government announced public sector wage guidelines of 10 per cent for the first year and 9 per cent for the second. These guidelines were quickly succeeded by more onerous controls with the *Compensation Stabilization Act* (Bill 28) on June 25, 1982, made retroactive to February. The Bill imposed compensation limits of 6 per cent in the first year and 5 per cent in the second, on 220,000 provincial, municipal, and regional public servants and employees of schools, hospitals, post-secondary education institutions, Crown corporations, government agencies and boards. Even senior management received no increase. Moreover, these limits could be lowered dependant upon historical relationship or special circumstances. Settlements had to meet employer's ability to pay, productivity, private sector wage levels, unemployment levels, and cost of living. A Compensation Stabilization Commissioner, appointed to review settlements, had the authority to make the final decision on acceptable agreements. The Bill provided Cabinet with the ability, *via regulations*, to amend compensation guidelines, prohibit increases, identify what is compensation and how increases are divided, and to prohibit reclassifications.

But this was not the end of British Columbia public sector compensation restraint legislation. Among the twenty-six regressive bills introduced with the budget on "Black Thursday," July 7, 1983, were additional measures dealing with wage restraint. The *Compensation Stabilization Amendment Act* (Bill 11), passed on October 21, changed the restraint guidelines and adjusted the Act's conditions—both in a much more perverse direction. New guidelines limited increases to a range of -5 to +5 per cent *for an indefinite period*. Additionally, the Bill made "the employer's ability to pay" the paramount consideration, effectively allowing Cabinet to set anyone's wages by adjusting the public sector's ability to pay.[21] The Bill also specifically allowed the government to unilaterally reduce compensation via regulation. No compensation plan could be implemented without being reviewed for conformity with the guidelines. It was also required that arbitrators should reconsider plans outside the guidelines. Appeals on wage decisions by the Commissioner were abolished. In effect, Bill 11 vitiated collective bargaining for public sector employees by setting up permanent wage controls under strict government authority.

In B.C., legislation affecting the framework of industrial relations proved to be even more damaging to trade union rights than restraint legislation. This began with the passage on August 4, 1982, of Bill 50, the *Labour Code Amendment Act*. While this Bill extended prohibitions on professional strike breaking to lockouts, picketing an ally of the employer was restricted by first requiring determination of ally status by the board and limits on picketing at a common site. These amendments were only the prelude to the proposals for permanent restrictions introduced on "Black Thursday" as part of a broader package of legislative assaults on the welfare state.

Bill 2, *Public Service Labour Relations Amendment Act*, although later withdrawn, proposed to legislate the British Columbia Government Employees' Union (BCGEU) master agreement out of existence, depriving government employees of the right to bargain over working conditions and the organization of work. The government would have gained the power to unilaterally eliminate positions superseding any procedural constraints on hiring, thus allowing for patronage appointments at all levels.

Bill 3, the *Public Sector Restraint Act*, assented to on October 21, 1983, permitted *all public sector employers* to terminate employees, without respect to job security, when there was not enough work, lack of funds, or changes or discontinuation of programmes and services. Since Cabinet could pass regulations implementing termination procedures, it gained the authority to unilaterally fire anyone under the guise of restraint. Bill 16, the *Employment Development Act*, passed at that time, empowered the government to prohibit strikes and/or picketing at any work site classified as an "economic development project." This so-called "job creation" programme also allowed the contracting-out of work normally performed by public service workers.

The final, major piece of labour legislation introduced in the October 21st budget was Bill 26, the *Employment Standards Amendment Act*. While eliminating the Employment Standards Board, this Act allowed the minimum standards of work to be overridden by private agreements between employer and employee. The Bill also widened the provisions by which an "interested person" (employer) could apply to have the provisions of a collective agreement set aside when the agreement expired and a new one not yet signed. Bill 26 represented a clear attack on trade union rights for both public and private sector workers as well as non-unionized employees. A few days after introducing this legislation, the British Columbia government proclaimed an amendment to the *Public Service Labour Relations Act* requiring, as of July 7, 1983, a mandatory strike vote by secret ballot for employees in a bargaining unit affected by a dispute.

The legislative assault of "Black Thursday" did not, as is well known, go unchallenged,[22] but was met by opposition of unprecedented scope and determination, which came together under the umbrella organization, Solidarity Coalition. In essence, it comprised two groupings: the Lower Mainland Solidarity Coalition, an amalgam of several hundred popular organizations, and the British Columbia Federation of Labour's Operation Solidarity, which also included independent unions like the Hospital Employees' Union and Confederation of Canadian Union affiliates. Countless imaginative local protests, as well as a series of massive demonstrations, effectively one-day general strikes of public sector workers, were held. On November 1, the BCGEU went out on strike, joined a week later by the unions in the education sector, as part of a plan for a phased escalation toward a general strike. This escalation was abruptly halted on November 13th by the infamous agreement struck in Kelowna between the Woodworkers' Jack Munro, on behalf of the British Columbia Federation, and Premier Bennett.

This "deal" certainly brought some relatively important victories. Bill 2 was withdrawn, "exemption clauses" allowing most public sector unions to escape Bill 3 were negotiated, and a seniority clause governing layoffs was won for the BCGEU, whose members were previously protected against any layoffs. This halted some of the originally-slated 1,600 firings. Nonetheless, it did not deflect the thrust of the government's initiative. The mass dismissal policy and the other "non-labour" budget measures that entailed sharply reduced education standards, together with the wholesale dismantling of civil rights protection and social services, especially for women, went ahead with but the vaguest of guarantees on "consultation" and non-reprisals against those who had participated in the Solidarity strikes. By March 1984, the government was claiming victory in its attempt to cut the civil service by 25 per cent.[23] While this claim entailed no little sleight-of-hand, it nevertheless was true that the job shifting that took place involved some civil service functions being transferred to non-union status or to more precarious situations in the charitable sector.

Perhaps most important, the legislative onslaught did not let up in British Columbia. On January 13, 1984, Workmen's Compensation Board rates were frozen at 1983 levels, saving employers millions at the expense of injured workers. More seriously, on May 16, 1984, the long-awaited *Labour Code Amendment Act* (Bill 28) substantially broadened the attack on trade union rights, especially in the private sector. The Bill's main features expressed "right-to-work" principles, extending the ability of employers to fight organizing drives and of employees to engage in decertification action, limiting the right to strike by banning political strikes and restricting secondary picketing. The Bill also allowed Cabinet to designate specific work sites as economic development projects, allowing for the suspension of collective agreements and banning strikes and walkouts on these sites. On August 25, 1984, this Bill was invoked on Vancouver's Expo 86 site, forcing unionized construction workers to work beside unorganized labour, notwithstanding a clause in their collective agreement which allowed them to refuse to do so.

In Saskatchewan, as in B.C., the overhaul of basic labour legislation was far more significant than the temporary wage restraint measures. Following the previous (NDP) government's resort to back-to-work legislation against hospital workers, the new Tory government announced guidelines limiting wage increases for public sector workers to 1 per cent below the rate of inflation. Immediately after its election in April 1982, the government had also introduced Bill 104, the *Trade Union Amendment Act*, passed on June 17, 1983. The many alterations introduced to the provincial industrial relations system were dramatic. They include widening the definition of employees considered management, and weakening the ability of unions to discipline members who cross picket lines or carry out anti-union activities. As well, the Bill made unions legal entities capable of suing or being sued. This was quite important as the amendments included an obligation for unions to provide a "duty of fair representation" and allow "for the application of the principles of natural justice" in disputes between employees and trade unions.

Greater government interference in internal union matters, especially concerning strikes, was also evident. Every employee, and employer, had to be given reasonable notice of union meetings and was required to receive forty-eight hours written notice of a strike or lockout. The Minister had to be notified of the date and time of a strike. As well as broadening the definition of who could vote in a strike ballot *to include non-union members of a bargaining unit*, the Labour Relations Board could now consider an application from the *employer, trade union, or affected employees* for the certification of a strike or ratification vote. After a strike continued for thirty days, these same groups could apply to the Board to have striking employees vote on the employer's final offer. Other substantial revisions also favoured management. A "free speech" clause extended management's ability to communicate with employees during organizing drives as well as during negotiations. Other revisions made certification requirements more onerous for unions. Finally, Bill 104 removed certain rights in a collective agreement in effect during a strike or lockout, such as seniority or recall rights and vacation leave. The Bill increased the fines provided for an unfair labour practice or contravention of the Act and made these applicable to the trade union where previously they were applicable only to individuals within a union.

With these sweeping changes to the structure of labour legislation, Bill 104 represented a substantial attack on trade unions and collective bargaining rights. After Bill 104, two additional pieces of legislation were passed in Saskatchewan affirming this trend. Assented to on December 12, 1983, Bill 24, *An Act to Repeal the Construction Industry Labour Relations Act*, undertook precisely what its name implies. Amendments to regulations under the *Public Sector Act*, in March 1984, changed compensation procedures and *reduced* the period for which maternity leave is available.

Unlike British Columbia and Saskatchewan, Alberta had never provided a legislative framework very favourable to labour and largely bypassed the extension of collective bargaining rights to public employees in the 1960s. Nonetheless, an already repressive situation took a sharp turn for the worse, in line with trends in Alberta's bordering provinces. What was in the wind was first revealed in Bill 11, the *Health Services Continuation Act* ordering striking Alberta nurses back to work, in March 1982. Dealing with some of the lowest-paid workers in the province, the government not only imposed binding arbitration but provided for union decertification and a prohibition on union members from union activity for a period of two years if the strike was not immediately stopped. A year later, on June 6, 1983, the *Labour Statutes Amendment Act* (Bill 44) was passed, permanently banning strikes by nurses and hospital workers and restricting the right to strike for other affected groups, notably, those (few) members of the Alberta Union of Public Employees who enjoyed this right. Under this Act, arbitrated collective agreements had to be submitted to a government-appointed tribunal which was required to consider government fiscal policy and general economic conditions in making awards, thereby enabling continual public sector restraint.

Under Bill 44, arbitrators themselves now had to consider factors such as government guidelines, employer's ability to pay, and non-union wages. The Bill effectively removed any pretence of fairness in the arbitration process: management was under no compulsion "to bargain in good faith" for it could refer the "collective bargaining" process to the arbitration board and it was the *Minister*, not the parties involved, who determined the items in dispute. Besides the compensation restraint and strike restrictions, Bill 44 had other sections of some importance. Similar to Quebec, employers could now suspend the deduction of union dues if a strike occurs. However, there were no penalties set for employers in lockouts.

The next step in Alberta's anti-labour campaign was Bill 110, which predominantly affected construction industry workers. The legislation came after intense lobbying from unionized contractors who had to pay substantially higher wages than non-union contractors. This Bill, the *Labour Relations Amendment Act*, was passed November 30, 1983, and would have allowed unionized construction companies to set up non-union subsidiaries to compete with other non-union companies not locked into high-wage contracts. However, extensive political protests kept the Bill on the shelf. In any case, the Alberta Federation of Labour felt that a Labour Relations Board ruling made Bill 110 unnecessary for unionized contractors.[24] The Board voided bridging clauses in collective agreements which entitled unionized employees to the conditions of the expired collective agreement until a new one was signed. This meant that employers could lock out workers for twenty-five hours, thus invalidating the expired contract and allowing them to rehire, according to the employers' own terms and conditions, former employees or to hire new, non-union ones. Subsequent rulings qualified this by declaring that the existing contract held until certification applications were ruled upon, thereby extending contracts thirty to ninety days past a legal lockout. As well, the Board termed contract-breaking lockouts an affront to the concept of joint-employer bargaining and ruled that employers were not free to change terms of the contracts without union agreement. Nevertheless, contractors continued to attempt to break unions or negate improvements in wages and conditions.

It is vital to stress that the wide-ranging attacks on trade union rights, which went well beyond the "temporary" aspect of wage restraint legislation, were not confined to Western Canada. Newfoundland introduced restrictions on the trade union rights of public sector employees, patterned after U.S.-style "right-to-work" legislation. Bill 59, *An Act to Amend the Public Service (Collective Bargaining) Act*, denied two thousand workers the right to join a union by broadening the basis for "managerial" exclusions. Besides making it more difficult to organize in the public sector, the Bill restricted union rights by placing new limits on collective action, including the prohibition of rotating strikes in the health sector. In Quebec, *An Act to Amend the Quebec Labour Code, the Code of Civil Procedures and Other Legislation* (Bill 72), restricting strikes in "essential services" was passed on the same day as Bill 70. The Act required public sector unions and employers to maintain essential services, primarily health and social services, during a strike. The onus was placed on the striking unions to assure a proper level of service. However, under the Act, the government was the final arbiter as to a sufficient level of service, and could outlaw the strike altogether if it believed this level of service was not being maintained.

It is perhaps indicative of how casual governments were becoming regarding restrictive changes in labour legislation that *An Act to Amend the Labour Relations Act* (Bill 75) passed through the Ontario Legislature in May and June 1984 with scarcely any debate and with the government neglecting to mention, let alone defend, the full extent of the changes. The amendments empowered the Ontario Labour Relations Board, in the case of illegal strikes, to act not only against trade unions and union officials but also "any person who has done or is threatening to do an act that the person knows or ought to know that, as a probably or reasonable consequence of the act, another person or persons will engage in an unlawful strike." The government explained to the legislature that the amendment was introduced to clarify the Labour Board's authority in the construction industry, permitting it to disallow one group of construction workers engaged in a dispute from closing down an entire site through "selective picketing." Without, however, explaining that it had done so, the government had amended the sections of the Act pertaining to the Board's powers in general, in the case of illegal strikes. By explicitly extending the Board's purview beyond union officials to activist rank-and-file members or to those who support them in illegal strikes, it not only made unofficial union groups (such as the health workers' council that helped organize the hospital workers' strikes in Ontario in 1980) subject to the Board's penalties, but also anyone who offered a financial, verbal or picketing encouragement or support. Although it is arguable that the Amendment merely clarifies the Board's powers, such a closing of potential loopholes still was indicative of current trends, particularly when the changes were slipped through as mundane matters rather than ones of democratic importance. The fact that both the press and the leadership of the industrial and political wings of the labour movement gave this legislation absolutely no attention was indicative of their lack of sensitivity to the coercive implications of such provisions.

Since coercion and consent are not mutually exclusive state strategies, a minor chord of reformism could still be heard in the controls period. The newly-elected NDP government in Manitoba passed amendments to the *Labor Relations Act* in 1982, which introduced extensive reforms, bringing Manitoba into line with other jurisdictions, and began a process of revamping the Manitoba *Labour Relations Act* (see Chapter Six).

In 1983, Ontario passed legislation imposing some limited restrictions on the use of "professional" strike breakers. At the federal level, the Liberal government, in its dying days in office, introduced a number of amendments to the Canadian Labour Code, enhancing minimum employment standards, individual worker rights and union recognition, specifying that the Rand formula be included in collective agreements. These reforms, while progressive and a welcome contrast to the overall repressiveness of the period, were neither extensive nor pathbreaking. Indeed, the federal legislation, save for the amendments enhancing union security, was not even proclaimed. As such, they can hardly be said to have muffled the coercive theme orchestrated by the state in the early 1980s. Those who thought the controls period was a temporary interruption of "free collective bargaining" were sadly mistaken.

CHAPTER 4

The Right to Strike: Freedom of Association and the Charter

In a modern state, law must not only correspond to the general economic conditions and be its expression, but must also be an *internally coherent* expression which does not, owing to inner contradictions, reduce itself to nought.... All the more so the more rarely it happens that a code of law is the blunt, unmitigated, unadulterated expression of the domination of a class—this in itself would offend the "conception of right." ... Thus to a great extent the course of the "development of right" only consists, first in the attempt to do away with contradictions arising from the direct translation of economic relations into legal principles, and to establish a harmonious system of law, and then in the repeated breaches made in this system by the influence and pressures of further economic development, which involves it in further contradictions ... The reflection of economic relations as legal principles is necessarily also a topsy-turvy one; it goes on without the person who is acting being conscious of it; the jurist imagines he is operating with *a priori* propositions, whereas they are really only economic reflexes, so everything is upside down. And it seems to me obvious that this inversion, which, so long as it remains unrecognized, forms an ideological conception, reacts in turn upon the economic basis, and may, within certain limits, modify it.

Frederich Engels [1]

We concentrated in the previous chapter on the restrictions which federal and provincial governments came to impose on labour by the early 1980s. We argued that these restrictions, in terms of substance and scope, signalled a transition from an era of consent in capital-labour relations to an era of coercion. We shall document in the next chapter how this trend lasted well past the moment when the "temporary" wage restraint legislation had run its course. In terms of its implications for labour rights in a liberal democracy such as Canada, the transition from consent to coercion in labour relations could not work itself through in a simple and straightforward fashion. The era of free collective bargaining had become enveloped in an ideological, juridical and international legal framework that could not simply be "reduced to nought" in the changing conditions of the 1980s. Indeed, the liberal-democratic legal principles of capitalist social relations in Canada were ostensibly given their most "internally coherent expression" with the constitutional entrenchment of the *Charter of Rights and Freedoms* in 1982. Section 2 of the new *Constitution Act, 1982* listed the "Fundamental Freedoms": (a) "freedom of conscience and religion;" (b) "freedom of thought, belief, opinion and expression;" (c) "freedom of peaceful assembly;" and (d) *"freedom of association."* These were guaranteed to *everyone*, except so far as section 1 made them "subject only to such reasonable limits as can be demonstrably justified in a free and democratic society."

And yet, it was a mark of the abstract, and to some extent cosmetic, nature of such an *a priori* guarantee of freedom of association that the framing of the Charter was so removed from the conjunctural conditions of class struggle in the early 1980s. As we have shown, by the time the Charter was proclaimed, the process of *ad hoc* state actions which arbitrarily undermined the *exercise* of freedom of association by large groups of workers was already well advanced. The harmonious system of constitutional law, the Charter established at an abstract level, was already being denied. In practice, what had come to the fore was the dissonance between the *guarantee* of freedom of association enunciated in the Charter and the increasing state *incursions* of this freedom, at least as exercised by workers.

By including "freedom of association" separately, as one of the four "Fundamental Freedoms," the Charter reflected the general development of the "conception of right" in liberal democratic discourse over the course of the twentieth century. The American *Bill of Rights* reflecting the legacy of eighteenth century politics and liberal discourse, makes no special mention of freedom of association. Rather, it received constitutional sanction via court interpretations (as regards workers, only some four decades ago) whereby freedom of association becomes an essential element to the realization of other specified freedoms, particularly, speech and assembly. Nevertheless, it was still significant that freedom of association remained undefined in the Canadian Charter. In promulgating the fundamental freedom of thought, belief, opinion and expression, it included freedom of the press and other media of communication. Notably, it was silent on whether freedom of association similarly included the essential means of making that freedom effective for working people, i.e. the associational rights to bargain and strike. Certain group rights were recognized in the Charter, above all the language and educational rights of French and English linguistic minorities and, albeit undefined, the rights and freedoms of the aboriginal peoples of Canada. To be sure, the coinage of liberal-democratic constitutional discourse uses a universal language of rights that obscures the class nature of capitalist societies. This largely accounts for the collective rights of subordinate classes generally being absent from declarations of rights. Certainly, it was still a mark of the Charter's conventional nature in this respect, that it did not advance the limits of liberal discourse regarding trade union rights—such as by following the examples set by the constitutions of France and Italy in the post-war period and the United Nations covenants on rights in the 1970s. At best, it could be said that the Charter was, at least, consistent, since it also refrained from expressly guaranteeing private property rights.

Given all this, for labour's right to bargain and strike to be an essential component of Canadian liberal democracy, it would require that the judiciary construe them as essential to freedom of association for workers. Despite certain equivocations during the constitutional debate, the actual practice of governments—in increasingly restricting the right to strike—could hardly instill confidence that the framers of the Charter expected the courts to interpret it in a manner constitutionally guaranteeing Canadian workers' rights to bargain collectively or strike. Even the "social justice" ideology, which Rand's famous ruling in 1946 (see Chapter 2) had enunciated to sustain and elaborate the legal enactments of the 1940s, bore a clear correspondence with the dominant ideological orientations of political elites at the time. Rand had accepted that "the predominance of capital over labour" was "unquestionable;" but he had interpreted the legislation of the 1940s to mean that the Canadian state had acknowledged that "the power of organised labour ... must be available to redress the balance of what is called social justice." The ideology emanating from the governments of the 1980s, in contrast, inevitably raised the question—since "trust and belief" in capital and the state, rather than "social justice," were the immediate order of the day—of what was *the point* of freedom of association for workers at all? For all its ringing abstract phrases, the Charter gave no positive guidance to answer this question.

Had it expressly included the right to strike, it would have served to limit the room to manoeuvre of the judiciary as well as of legislatures. But, in any case, there was a loophole, cynically crafted by the Attorneys General of Saskatchewan, Ontario and the Federal government in their infamous middle-of-the-night meeting in the kitchen of Ottawa's Conference Centre. The "notwithstanding clause" (Section 33) at the tail end of the Charter allows governments to pass legislation which specifically declares than an Act is not subject to its fundamental freedoms or equality rights provisions. (Such a declaration ceases to have effect after a five-year period, but the "notwithstanding" declaration can be re-enacted.) Thus, even if the Canadian courts were to give a broad and generous interpretation to freedom of association, it was by no means guaranteed that governments determined to restrict the rights of labour would necessarily adhere to them. To be fair, it could be argued that the "notwithstanding clause" also gives governments an escape clause if the courts construed the Charter in such a way as to protect capital's property rights. Given the orientations of Canadian governments in the 1980s, that was a rather abstract concern. In contrast stood the all too palpable contradiction of the federal and provincial governments' behaviour with respect to labour's rights in the 1980s: incorporating a freedom of association provision in the *Charter of Rights and Freedoms*, cheek by jowl with legislation effectively removing the right to strike and free collective bargaining from public and para-public employees. This immediately threw into the lap of the courts the responsibility for re-establishing a semblance of coherence to the rule of law in Canada in the sphere of labour relations.

Freedom of Association and the ILO

Until the Charter's entrenchment in the Canadian Constitution, the most ready avenue of juridical appeal by Canadian unions—in light of federal and provincial governments' violations of the principle of freedom of association—was to the International Labour Organization, a United Nations tripartite agency (composed of business, labour and government representatives), of which Canada has been a member since 1919. However, Canada has never had a particularly sterling record when it came to ratifying ILO Conventions (having to date ratified only 26 of 160 Conventions). This, in good part, is because such ratification requires unanimous provincial consent; although, it is questionable how much priority the federal government assigned to securing such assent. The last one the Canadian Government ratified was *Convention (No. 87) Concerning Freedom of Association and Protection of the Right to Organize, 1948*, in March 1972. The general principles of this Convention, as interpreted by the ILO's Committee on Freedom of Association, establish that freedom of association as it pertains to unions (public as well as private sector) must encompass the freedom to bargain collectively and to strike. The unanimous consent finally obtained, in 1972, from all the provincial governments for ratifying this Convention, may be taken as the symbolic high water mark of the era of "free collective bargaining."

In the ensuing years, the Canadian state's shift toward legislative interventions against labour rights led to increasing complaints by Canadian unions to the ILO's Committee on Freedom of Association. Whereas only four complaints came from Canada over the two decades from 1954 to 1973, no less than nineteen complaints were registered from 1974-85. If we compare Canada with the leading "Group of Seven" capitalist countries, Canada has become the cause of more complaints than any other, despite its much smaller population: from accounting for less than four per cent of all complaints registered against these countries in the 1954-73 period, Canada accounted for one-third of total complaints from 1974-85. Still, one must be very careful with these comparisons: they must not be taken on their own as showing that any one government restricts union freedoms more than another. Such complaints reflect a dialectic between state behaviour and the inclinations of trade unions in individual countries to make use of the ILO's capacity for moral suasion against governments. This inclination to appeal to the ILO will depend on a given labour movement's attitude to that body, its general approach to litigation, as well as the availability of other juridical avenues of appeal regarding incursions against freedom of association. A growing number of complaints to the ILO is only *suggestive* that something untoward is afoot in the country in question in the view of its labour movement, indicative primarily of a growing dissent between it and the state. What is significant about Table V, therefore, is less the comparisons with other countries than the absolute increase in the number of Canadian complaints since 1974.

TABLE V
Complaints of Violations of Trade Union Rights Filed with the
ILO Against the Group of Seven Capitalist Countries [2]

Countries	1954-73		1974-85	
	No.	%	No.	%
Canada	4	3	19	32
France	31	25	5	8
Italy	5	4	2	3
Japan	8	7	15	25
United Kingdom	55	45	11	19
U.S.A.	16	13	6	10
West Germany	4	3	1	2
Total	123	100	59	99

(Percentages reflect rounding.)

The ILO is certainly not a body quick to condemn its member states. It keeps a very close eye on retaining the membership of those many regimes which by no stretch of the imagination could be designated as anything other than authoritarian—whether capitalist or communist. For instance, it was an unusual act for the ILO to send a fact-finding mission to Poland, as it did after the government's repression of the Solidarity movement in the early 1980s. When the ILO issued a critical report, [3] Poland withdrew from the organization—which is likely what most other authoritarian regimes would have done had the ILO been asked, or moved similarly, to condemn them. Even regarding liberal democracies, where it has more scope, the ILO has been inclined to give governments the benefit of the doubt in respect to "temporary" measures (such as statutory incomes policy programmes) which restrict the right to bargain and strike; and it has accepted that the right to strike for workers in "essential services" can be prohibited on the grounds that strike activity might endanger public health and safety.

It is not surprising, therefore, that the outcome of Canadian union complaints to the ILO has been a very mixed bag. So extreme was the federal government's action in imposing back-to-work legislation on the postal workers in 1978, (leading to the imprisonment of J.C. Parrot) that even the ILO felt moved to slap the Canadian government's wrists gently for substituting *ad hoc* restrictive interventions of this nature, rather than founding its policy "on permanent legislation respecting the principles of freedom of association."[4] Moreover, the Freedom of Association Committee had also found, in 1980, that Alberta's general ban on strikes for provincial public employees had defined "essential services" too broadly to conform with the principle of freedom of association.[5] As we have seen, Alberta stood out among Canadian jurisdictions for grimly resisting the extension of trade union rights to public employees. Far from adhering to the ILO ruling, it went even further, in 1983, by enacting Bill 44, which extended the denial of the right to strike to nurses and other para-public employees. When it came to other complaints, the ILO was reluctant to be critical. It did not sustain a complaint, in 1979, with regard to Nova Scotia's infamously cynical Michelin Bill. When the federal "6 and 5" legislation and Quebec's Law 70 of 1982-83 were brought before the ILO, it stated that they did not contravene freedom of association; albeit adding the "condition" that these laws remain exceptional in nature, without exceeding a reasonable period and accompanied by safeguards protecting workers' living standards.[6] Given the federal wage-restraint legislation was in force for over half the decade 1975-85, that non-compensatory issues were also removed from bargaining in the 1982 legislation, and that there was no recourse to independent arbitration, it was a typically timorous ruling.

So extensive was the assault on freedom of association by federal and provincial governments in the early 1980s, and so numerous and plausible the complaints brought by Canadian unions, that the ILO, in 1985, took the unusual step (the first time since its founding in 1919) of sending a special study and information mission to examine the complaints brought against the Ontario, Alberta and Newfoundland legislation passed in 1982 and 1983. On the basis of the mission's report, the ILO ruled in November 1985 that the Alberta and Newfoundland legislation (Bills 44 and 57 respectively) and, to a lesser extent that of Ontario (Bill 179), had indeed violated trade union freedoms. This set of critical rulings, dramatized by the mission to Canada, received a good deal of publicity. But it hardly stood alone.

If we look at the recent ILO rulings on Canada overall, it is indeed remarkable how many have actually been sustained. In the case of "temporary" wage restraint legislation, Nova Scotia, Ontario and Alberta were deemed to have transgressed fundamental union freedoms by restricting the scope of negotiation and arbitration and by unilaterally modifying collective agreements. British Columbia was deemed to have established a restraint system that amounted to an unjustifiably prolonged, if not actually permanent, suspension of fundamental union freedoms; moreover, it was found to have created a situation whereby benefits under collective agreements could actually be lower than those established by employment standards. By requiring adherence to government fiscal policies in Alberta and British Columbia, restrictions on arbitrators' independence were also found to infringe on the principles of collective bargaining, as was the B.C. provision requiring the prior approval of collective agreements by a government-appointed Commissioner before they came into force. Most notable of all, perhaps, is that no less than six provinces (British Columbia, Alberta, Ontario, Quebec, Nova Scotia and Newfoundland) have all been found by the ILO to be contravening the freedom of association provision of Convention 87 by virtue of the generality of their *permanent* restrictions on public and para-public sector workers' right to strike. [7]

The tone of the ILO rulings are invariably diplomatic, expressing "concern" and suggesting appropriate "amendment," but a degree of exasperation has crept in even here. As one ruling pertaining to Nova Scotia put it:

... the Committee of Freedom of Association recalls that the right to strike could be restricted in the strict sense of the term, i.e. services whose interruption would endanger the existence or well-being of the whole or part of the population. The ban on strike activity for employees of the Art

Gallery, Boxing Authority and Communications and Information Centre appears to the Committee to go far beyond this criterion. [8]

Canadian Judicial Review

The ILO decisions have generally been ignored by Canadian governments. This stands as sorry testament to the degree of dissonance between Canada's formal adherence to international declarations on labour rights and their actual embodiment in the practices of the Canadian state. What of the guarantee of freedom of association now established in the Canadian Constitution itself? Canadian governments could hardly ignore this so readily. As governmental transgressions of the right to strike and to bargain collectively followed one after the other, Canadian unions, despite their initial disdain for involving themselves in Charter debates, increasingly appealed to the Canadian courts, hoping to secure the guarantee of freedom of association that the Charter now constitutionally established on grounds similar to those that Justice Rand had offered forty years earlier.

It must be said that despite the ideological and juridical importance of Rand's 1946 ruling, the pro-employer bias of most judges could hardly be missed over the ensuing decades. As such, in the conditions of the 1980s, it could have been expected that most Canadian judges could be counted on to endorse whatever restrictions parliament or provincial legislatures imposed. Often enough, they had found ways to employ their own "judgemade" doctrines to invent or manipulate restrictions on labour and had used nonconstitutional juridical review to fashion expansive interpretations of the law to benefit employers (above all through the ready use of injunctions). However, freedom of association was not within their constitutional frame of reference as a means of limiting government actions until 1982. It was never clear whether this judicial bias extended, on their part, to challenging the fundamentals. The legislative assault on unions that accompanied the Charter's introduction ensured that the answer would not be too long in coming.

However unlikely it was that the courts would interpret the Charter generously for workers, one should never minimize the effect of judicial review in a liberal democracy. Whether the courts—ultimately responsible for overseeing the coherence of a legal system—would sustain a legislative assault on free collective bargaining in the face of the embodiment of freedom of association in the Constitution was crucial; a great deal depended on the outcome. Above all, would the courts sanction the "temporary" and *ad hoc* incursions by the state against (mainly public sector) workers' rights *with such a restrictive interpretation of freedom of association* that an even broader coercive industrial relations regime in Canada would be facilitated? Would they garb it with an ideological and juridical coherence that would give it the kind of permanence characterizing not a mere moment in the life of a society, but a whole era?

It was a measure of the dissonance in Canada's constitutional labour law, created in the 1980s, that the judiciary, far from immediately providing a semblance of coherence, was revealed to be in a state of confusion itself for some time. From 1983-87, the courts did not resolve, but rather mirrored and reproduced that dissonance through a cacophony of contradictory judgements. In the first instance, the Divisional Court of the Ontario High Court ruled in 1983 (in the *Broadway Manor* case testing the constitutionality of Ontario's *Inflation Restraint Act*) that legislative disposal of collective bargaining rights and of the right to strike, by cynically extending collective agreements beyond their termination, was unconstitutional. Overturning a decision by the Ontario Labour Relations Board endorsing this practice, the three judges of the High Court unanimously held that the Charter guarantee of freedom of association extended to the activities of trade unions. As Justice Galligan put it:

> Freedom of association must include freedom to engage in conduct which is reasonably consonant with the lawful objectives of the association. The purpose of an association of workers in a union is to advance their common interests. If they are not free to take such lawful steps that they see as reasonable to advance those interests, including bargaining and striking, then as a practical matter their association is barren and useless.[9]

Even if this argument only recalled a long-established principle (going back in Canada to 1872), these were still heady words, reflecting what Justice Galligan termed the need for "a large and liberal construction" of freedom of association judicially. It seemed to suggest the reality, and the importance, of a degree of relative autonomy the courts had from both government and capital. Despite the strong words, the ruling itself had little strength. It is not unusual for judges to award one side a victory in principle, while giving the other the substantive victory. The court only narrowed the range of "permanent exceptionalism." It found that the *Inflation Restraint Act* as a whole could stand, on the grounds that the imposition of temporary, statutory wage restraint was a political judgement consonant with the exceptional infringements of the fundamental freedoms, allowed for under s. 1 of the Charter. As Justice Smith said: "... it is not an unreasonable limit upon freedom of association to contain compensation for a limited period of time and hence the right to strike, once a political decision is made to bring inflation down." It was only that aspect of the Act, Section 13(b), which arbitrarily froze the pattern of union organization and also restricted bargaining over non-monetary matters (via the blanket extension of pre-existing collective agreements) that was unconstitutional. Thus, given that statutory wage controls had been in effect for more years than not since 1975, in Ontario as in most Canadian jurisdictions, the court put its stamp on "permanent exceptionalism" by endorsing the primacy of political judgements over freedom of association when it came to wage restraint.

This is not to say that the aspect of the judgement that limited the range of permanent exceptionalism only to "temporary" wage restraint was unimportant. It not only challenged the much broader nature of the extant shift to coercion, but also implicitly challenged such special restrictions for public servants on the right to bargain and strike as had been applied in most Canadian jurisdictions. However, the strength of the judgement was further vitiated even in this respect, as the Alberta government immediately displayed the utility of Section 33 of the Charter for governments that would not brook the relative autonomy of the courts with respect to positive interpretations of labour's rights.

In the wake of the *Broadway Manor* judgement, Premier Lougheed declared his government would use the "notwithstanding clause" to ensure that Alberta's public sector workers could still be denied the right to strike. But would such an open conflict between the legislature and the courts really be necessary? This could not be ascertained on the basis of the *Broadway Manor* judgement alone, and the Alberta government immediately initiated a reference to the Alberta Court of Appeal whereby an advisory opinion was sought on the constitutionality of those provisions of the province's *Public Services Employees Act, Labour Relations Act,* and *Police Officers' Collective Bargaining Act,* which denied the right to strike and imposed a system of compulsory arbitration.

The majority of the Alberta Court of Appeal responded with a judgement that directly contradicted the *Broadway Manor* ruling in Ontario. [10] The provisions of the Charter had to be interpreted in a "broad and liberal" manner, but not in an "extreme or extravagant" way either. The court was not persuaded that prohibition of strikes and the imposition of compulsory arbitration limited public employees' freedom of association or ability to bargain collectively in a meaningful manner. In any case, a measure of restraint was required in judicial review. As Justice Kerans put it, the courts should not interpret the Charter's guarantee of freedom of association as providing protection to "all actions by all groups to carry out all group purposes." The arbitrariness of this interpretation should not be overlooked. When it came to a judgement upholding the prerogatives of the Law Society of Alberta in 1986, [11] Justice Kerans took the view that "... the special status given to the freedom of association in Canada reflects our tradition about the importance for a free and democratic society of non-governmental organization. In my view, the freedom includes the freedom to associate with others in protection of Charter protected rights and also those other rights which—in Canada—are thought so fundamental as not to need formal expression." Among these, he included the right to "gain a livelihood." Beneath such high sounding *a priori* principles, rather narrow class interests were at play. Sauce for the gander (lawyers) was not to be sauce for the goose (public employees).

Just how crucial the issue at stake was, not only for the Alberta government, but virtually for the Canadian state as a whole at the time, was seen when *the Attorney General of Canada and Attorneys General of no less than seven other provinces intervened on the side of Alberta* when this judgement was appealed to the Supreme Court of Canada by the Alberta Union of Provincial Employees, the Alberta International Firefighters' Association and the Canadian Union of Public Employees. (Manitoba, where the NDP was in office, intervened on the side of the unions; New Brunswick alone stayed out of this juridical fracas.) It took until April of 1987 for the Supreme Court's long-delayed judgement to be rendered, and by this time, an even broader array of lower court judgements had accumulated. A clear inflection toward an interpretation that disadvantaged trade union freedoms appeared in these judgements, but it is important to emphasize that they only sustained what governments were doing to disadvantage labour. It was not a matter of the courts *versus* the Attorneys General and their legislatures; it was the Attorneys General, the legislatures and the courts *versus labour.*

In March 1984, the Federal Court, responding to a Public Service Alliance of Canada challenge to the federal "6 and 5" legislation, explicitly ruled that freedom of association did not include the right to strike for trade unions and endorsed temporary, statutory wage restraint as a "valid objective," despite its effects on organization and bargaining over non-monetary matters and despite its application to public servants alone. This decision was upheld by the Federal Court of Appeals in June 1984: the legislation had deprived public servants of the right to bargain collectively, but this did not impinge on freedom of association.[12] Justice Mahoney found that the Charter "protects neither the objects of the association nor the means of attaining those objects...." Justice Macreau added: "I fail to see on the basis of which rule of construction, however liberal it may be, one can be able to give to the words 'freedom of association' a meaning broad enough to include the right to strike."

In this respect, the federal appeals court was explicitly following an earlier judgement by the B.C. Court of Appeal that year, where the majority concluded that the Charter's guarantees of freedom of association and expression could not be used to secure the right of workers to engage in picketing (the *Dolphin Delivery* case).[13] Restrictive interpretations of freedom of association were adopted by trial division courts in Newfoundland, Manitoba and Nova Scotia as well.[14] Nevertheless, the Ontario Court of Appeals in October 1984, without striking down the judgement of the Divisional Court the year before, completely sidestepped the constitutional issue and argued that the lower court had been wrong to base its decision on the constitutional grounds of freedom of association.[15] Yet, in 1985, the Saskatchewan Court of Appeal in examining a case of back-to-work legislation rejected in very strong terms these interpretations (the *Dairy Workers* case).[16] The majority ruling broadly returned to the reasoning that underlined the initial *Broadway Manor* judgement in Ontario and emphasized the connection between freedom of association for workers and the freedom to bargain collectively and strike. To be faithful to the Charter's guarantees, the courts had to give the fundamental freedoms a "generous interpretation ... suitable to give to individuals the full measure of them."

The Saskatchewan government took note. Not deterred from legislating its public employees back to work in a dispute in 1986, it invoked the "notwithstanding clause" of the Charter to override the expansive interpretation of its guarantee of freedom of association.[17] In 1982, the NDP Government of Saskatchewan had played a key role in inserting the notwithstanding clause into the Charter. It had occasionally justified its defence of parliamentary sovereignty on the grounds that this would ensure that the courts could not intervene against legislation undermining capital's property rights. As it turned out, it was to be a Saskatchewan government, the Devine Conservatives having defeated the NDP in the interim (albeit in suspending the right to strike through back-to-work legislation the new government was not breaking with precedent set by the NDP itself), that was to be the first to use the notwithstanding clause selectively to undermine a judicial ruling in favour of labour's rights.

The Supreme Court Decision

It was left to the Supreme Court to provide coherence to all this juridical dissonance. An important sign of the way the wind was blowing on the Supreme

Court appeared in December 1986, when it dismissed an appeal of the *Dolphin Delivery* ruling on picketing. This ruling had been challenged, not on the grounds of freedom of association, but freedom of expression, which had to take into account private property rights. So the issue was only directly addressed on April 9, 1987, when the Supreme Court finally offered a set of simultaneous judgements on appeals on the *Alberta Reference*, the *Public Service Alliance of Canada* challenge to the "6 and 5" legislation and the *Dairy Workers* case.[18]

The judgement rendered in *Alberta Reference*, since the Alberta legislation provided the broadest and most permanent example of the denial of the rights to strike and bargain collectively, took centre stage. The decision in this case would frame the response given by the court to the question of the validity of more *ad hoc* and temporary restrictions of the kind involved in the back-to-work legislation case and "temporary" statutory wage-restraint cases. The majority judgement, written by Justice Le Dain, was a shockingly brief one, running to only three substantive paragraphs—the reasoning short in elegance as it was in social justice:

> The constitutional guarantee of freedom of association on s. 2(d) of the *Canadian Charter of Rights and Freedoms* does not include, in the case of a trade union, a guarantee of the right to bargain collectively and the right to strike. In considering the meaning that must be given to freedom of association in s. 2(d) of the Charter, it is essential to keep in mind that this concept must be applied to a wide range of associations or organizations of a political, religious, social or economic nature, with a very wide variety of objects, as well as activity by which these objects may be pursued. It is in this larger perspective, and not simply with regard to the perceived requirements of a trade union, however important they may be, that one must consider the implications of extending the concept of freedom of association, to the right to engage in particular activity on the ground that the activity is essential to give an association meaningful existence.
>
> In considering whether it is reasonable to ascribe such a sweeping intention to the Charter, the premise that without such additional constitutional protection the guarantee of freedom of association would be a meaningless and empty one must be rejected. Freedom of association is particularly important for the exercise of other fundamental freedoms, such as freedom of expression and freedom of conscience and religion. These afford a wide scope for protected activity in association. Moreover, the freedom to work for the establishment of an association, to belong to an association, to maintain it, and to participate in its lawful activity without penalty is not to be taken for granted. That is indicated by its express recognition and protection in labour relations legislation. It is a freedom that has been suppressed in varying degrees from time to time by totalitarian regimes. What is at issue here is not the importance of freedom of association in this sense but whether particular activity of an association in pursuit of its objects is to be constitutionally protected or left to be regulated by legislative policy. The rights for which constitutional protection is sought—the modern rights to bargain collectively and to strike,

involving correlative duties or obligations resting on an employer—are not fundamental rights or freedoms. They are the creation of legislation, involving a balance of competing interests in a field which has been recognized by the courts as requiring special expertise. It is surprising that, in an area in which this Court has affirmed a principle of judicial restraint in the review of administrative action, this Court should be considering the substitution of its judgement for that of the legislature by constitutionalizing in general and abstract terms rights which the legislature has found it necessary to define and qualify in various ways according to the particular field of labour relations involved. The resulting necessity of applying s. 1 of the Charter to a review of particular legislation in this field demonstrates the extent to which the Court becomes involved in a review of legislative policy for which it is not really fitted.

Thus, was the constitutional issue of the right to strike and bargain collectively disposed. Note that there are but three reasons offered. The first involves an equation of working-class association with all other associations, adopting a haunting silence on the capitalist and class nature of Canadian society. The second explicitly denies that freedom of association involves a distinct and separate conception of freedom from the others enumerated in the Charter, despite the fact that the Charter specifically recognizes it as such. The Court has now rendered it an adjunct to the other fundamental freedoms, such as freedom of expression or belief. The constitutional guarantee of freedom of association is reduced to what you can say or think, omitting what is necessary for workers to do about their subordinate status *vis-à-vis* their employers. Finally, the Court reasoned—with no little dissimulation regarding judicial activism benefitting employers *before* the Charter, and despite its rulings in other contexts affirming its new activist role *under* the Charter—that what the legislature granted, the legislature can take away. (There was little to be exultant about in terms of this sudden judicial modesty in the face of parliamentary democracy and the "specialized" field of labour relations. It was on such grounds, if we may be permitted to engage in a *reductio ad absurdum* for a moment, that judges excused themselves, when Hitler came to power constitutionally, from objecting to his government's dismantling of the independent trade union movement—and later from much worse.) All this was done without so much as a bow to the fact that for a century the courts had recognized that workers could legally use their collective economic power in certain circumstances.[19] Nor, extremely unconventionally, was any reference made to the international conventions and covenants to which Canada is a signatory.

Having rendered this blunt judgement, the Court felt no need to comment on specific "exceptional" abrogations of the right to strike and bargain collectively, such as were on appeal before it. Indeed, the ruling did not even deign to address one of the important questions raised by the *Alberta Reference* itself, which pertained to s. 2(2) of the *Police Officers' Act*. This section explicitly forbids police officers from becoming a member of a trade union or of an organization directly or indirectly affiliated with a trade union. The majority ruling had nothing at all to say about this; despite the grand claims it made for the importance of freedom of association, even short of the right to strike and bargain collectively, and despite adducing Canadian labour legislation guarantees in respect of workers' freedom of association as proof that Canada was not a "totalitarian state." That such a critical decision should have been rendered in such a sloppy manner was a sad commentary on the Canadian judiciary. An elegant judgement it was not.

For those who see liberal democracy as transcending class domination simply by virtue of the citizenship rights of individual workers, this judgement may suffice. For those who see liberal democracy simply as majority rule through parliamentary sovereignty, with citizens' direct involvement in decision making limited to participating in elections every four-or-so years and engaging in pressure group activities, this judgement may again suffice. And for those who trust the decisions of party politicians and bureaucrats more than they trust the decision of judges, the judgement may also suffice. But, those who note, with the Court itself, that the suppression of freedom of association for workers has been a litmus test of totalitarian regimes, will wonder at the Court's *sang froid*, and disturbing illogic, as it contrasts Canadian democracy with "totalitarianism" by citing Canadian labour legislation—and then immediately gives governments full and untrammelled lease to abrogate the rights upon which that legislation is based.

As we already recalled, Justice Rand had cited "the history of the past century" as demonstrating "that the power of organised labour had to be available to redress the balance of what is called social justice." The struggles by workers to organize at that time were seen by Rand to connect with the statist notions of reformist "gradualism" of his day, sanctioning labour laws designed to harmonize the capital-labour relationship to the end of securing social order in a class society. Rand had recognized as a fundamental condition of capitalist society that whereas the power of employers lay in their ownership and/or control of the means of labour; the power of those who sold their labour lay in their collective organization, and he regarded labour legislation as an historic institutionalization of working-class rights in a capitalist democracy. However, in 1987 the Supreme Court grimly refused the opportunity opened by the Charter to constitutionally sanction this.

Notably, in a concurring and much longer judgement, Justice McIntyre laid bare a deeper reasoning, one much more telling of the impulses—in the current conjuncture of capitalism and class struggle—that lay behind the legislative assault on trade unions and its judicial sanctioning. At one level, McIntyre's ruling epitomized a judicial frame of mind which portrays the world in a topsy-turvy fashion, concealing behind *a priori* notions the economic and political developments that give rise to such judgements and, indeed, so often motivate the decisions of judges. The primary reason advanced by Justice McIntyre for rejecting the position that freedom of association for workers necessarily entailed the right to bargain and strike was that guarantees in the Charter, apart from aboriginal rights, were individual rather than group rights. Accordingly, while freedom of association advanced many group interests and could obviously not be exercised by an individual alone, nevertheless, freedom of association was only -

... a freedom belonging to the individual and not to the group formed through its exercise ... The only basis on which it is contended that the Charter enshrines the right to strike is that of freedom of association. Collective bargaining is a group concern, a group activity, but the group can exercise only the constitutional right of its individual members on behalf of those members. If the right asserted is not found in the Charter for the individual, it cannot be implied for the group merely by the fact of association. It follows as well that the rights of the individual members of the group cannot be enlarged merely by the fact of association.

But at another level, Justice McIntyre revealed that beneath such *a priori* assertions regarding the primacy of individual rights and the redundancy of subordinate class rights, lay more pragmatic and prosaic considerations.

Labour law ... is based upon a political and economic compromise between organized labour—a very powerful socio -economic force—on the one hand, and employers of labour—an equally powerful socio-economic force—on the other. The balance between the two forces is delicate and the public-at-large depends for its security and welfare on the maintenance of that balance.... The whole process is inherently dynamic and unstable. Care must be taken then in considering whether constitutional protection should be given to one aspect of this dynamic and evolving process while leaving the other subject to the social pressures of the day. Great changes—economic, social, and industrial—are afoot, not only in Canada and North America, but as well in other parts of the world. Changes in the Canadian national economy, the decline in resource-based as well as heavy industries, the changing patterns of international trade and industry, have resulted in great pressures to reassess the traditional approaches to economic and industrial questions, including questions of labour law and policy.... To intervene in that dynamic process at this early stage by implying constitutional protection for the right to strike, would, in my view, give to one of the contending forces an economic weapon removed from and made immune, subject to s. 1, to legislative control which could go far toward freezing the development of labour relations and curtailing that process of evolution necessary to meet the changing circumstances of a modern society in the modern world.[20]

It will be noted that like Justice Rand forty years before, Justice McIntyre did not shrink from making explicit reference to capital and labour as the primary socio-economic forces at work in society. Justice Rand openly recognized that capital was structurally the dominant and labour, the subordinate force in "a society whose economic life has private enterprise as its dynamic." Justice McIntyre, by contrast, referred to capital merely as "employers" and treated capital and labour as "two equally powerful" socio-economic forces. Moreover, though McIntyre said much about "dynamics," and was not unperceptive regarding those at work in our time, he was silent when it came to relating the dynamics to private enterprise. Still, McIntyre, no less than Rand, certainly recognized that the evolution of labour legislation reflected delicate shifts in the balance between capital and labour. Rather, what McIntyre did was make more explicit the effect of the Court's majority ruling. It provided a judicial rationale for a state now concerned less with securing "social harmony" in labour relations and more with undoing the collective power of labour organization in the context of the global, as well as domestic, capitalist restructuring of our time.

If McIntyre's judgement was more obscure than Rand's, this was, perhaps, not only due to personal factors, but also to the ideological effects of post-war collective bargaining in concealing the class relationships and private profit-driven dynamics of a capitalist society. Moreover, such is the relative autonomy of the judiciary in a liberal democracy, that it cannot be said that this particular decision by the Supreme Court was inevitable. Indeed, it was not unanimous and there were two dissenting opinions—by Chief Justice Dickson and by Justice Bertha Wilson. Their dissent, as carefully reasoned and exhaustive as the majority judgement was pre-emptory, cited foreign jurisprudential authorities in a balanced and considered fashion, including experts in international law. The Chief Justice came to a chilling, and in our view incontrovertible, conclusion: *"If freedom of association only protects the joining together of persons for common purposes, but not the pursuit of the very activities for which the association was formed, then the freedom is indeed legalistic, ungenerous, indeed vapid."*

In the Chief Justice's view, the majority judgement had rendered the Charter's explicit and independent guarantee of freedom of association superfluous: "the express conferral of a freedom of association is unnecessary if all that is intended is to give effect to the collective enjoyment of other freedoms." Nor was it only individual political rights that were protected by the Charter:

> Just as the individual is incapable of resisting political domination without the support of persons with similar values, so too is he or she, in isolation incapable of resisting domination, over the long term, in many other aspects of life.... Freedom of association is most essential in those circumstances where the individual is liable to be prejudiced by the actions of some larger and more powerful entity, like the government or an employer ... it has enabled those who would otherwise be vulnerable and ineffective to meet on more equal terms the power and strength of those with whom their interests interact and, perhaps, conflict....
>
> There will ... be occasions when no analogy involving individuals can be found for associational activity, or when a comparison between groups and individuals fails to capture the essence of a possible violation of associational rights. This is precisely the situation in this case. There is no individual equivalent to the right to strike. The refusal to work by one individual does not parallel a collective refusal to work.... The legislative purpose which will render legislation invalid is the attempt to preclude associational conduct because of its concerted or associational nature....
>
> The role of association has always been vital as a means of protecting the essential needs and interests of working people. Throughout history, workers have associated to overcome their vulnerability as individuals to the strength of their employers. The capacity to bargain collectively has long been recognized as one of the integral and primary functions of

associations of working people. While trade unions also fulfil other important social, political and charitable functions, collective bargaining remains vital to the capacity of individual employees to participate in ensuring fair wages, health and safety precautions and equitable and humane working conditions. [21]

The Rand spirit is not hard to discern here. Indeed, it was precisely the retention, and constitutional sanctioning, of the general framework of the old labour relations regime that Dickson's judgement was designed to secure within the framework of the Charter. He did not claim that these considerations rendered invalid the legal regulation of collective bargaining and the right to strike: "... the view that certain rights and freedoms cannot be protected by the Charter's provisions because they are the subject of statutory regulation is premised on a fundamental misconception of judicial review under a written constitution." What was at issue in the *Alberta Reference* was not the general labour laws of Alberta, which permitted strike activity and collective bargaining subject to statutory regulation; it was "the substitution of an entirely different mechanism for resolving labour disputes for particular employees, and one which does not merely regulate the freedom to strike but abrogates it entirely." On these grounds, the Alberta legislation which aimed at a blanket prohibition of strikes for public employees or prohibited trade union membership itself were to be deemed unconstitutional. But under s.1 of the Charter, infringements on the right to strike and bargain collectively, could be deemed as falling within the "reasonable limits" to which the fundamental freedoms were subject in a "free and democratic society," on the condition that the onus of proof that a limit was valid fell on the party seeking such a limit.

The relatively generous interpretation of freedom of association rendered by Justice Dickson should not, however, obscure *its* limits. In fact, Justice Dickson, in the tradition of the old regime, was prepared to validate a fairly broad set of grounds upon which such limits could be imposed. He accepted the ILO's definition of "essential services," but, since the Attorney General of Alberta did not adduce any evidence why all public service employees, hospital workers, firefighters and police officers were "essential," the onus of proof that fell on the Alberta government was not satisfied. Nor could the government assume absolute authority to determine at what point a matter had to go to arbitration. On the other hand, the Chief Justice had no difficulty in accepting that statutory limits could be imposed on matters for arbitration, or that statutory requirements that fiscal policy be considered by arbitrators did not compromise the fairness of arbitration.

Similarly, in Dickson's view, the "important leadership role of the federal government in a fight against inflation" justified the imposition of statutory wage controls on the federal public sector under s. 1 of the Charter. "A pressing and substantial social concern need not amount to an emergency.... In my opinion, courts must exercise considerable caution when confronted with difficult questions of economic policy." He showed little such caution, however, when he went on to cite and endorse explicitly the ideology advanced by the Trudeau government in portraying statutory restraint on public sector workers as an example for voluntary restraint by all workers. Even so, the Chief Justice was not ready to endorse the wage control legislation in full, finding, as the Ontario High Court had done, that the removal of the right to strike over non-compensatory issues, as well as the right to submit such issues to arbitration, was not a justifiable infringement on freedom of association. Indeed, this "represented a profound intrusion into the associational freedom of workers, one which bore no apparent connection to the objectives of an anti-inflation programme. The *Public Sector Compensation Restraint Act* has swept away virtually the full range of collective bargaining activities of federal employees, seemingly without any thought as to whether such draconian measures were necessary."

But Dickson's inclination was still to endorse, under s. 1, a very broad sphere for governmental practice of "permanent exceptionalism." It was highly significant that the Chief Justice defended the back-to-work legislation of the Saskatchewan government in the *Dairy Workers* case in the following terms:

To be blind to the economic harm which may ensue from work stoppages would be to freeze into the constitution a particular system of industrial relations. Although, as yet, it would appear that Canadian legislatures have not yet discovered an alternative mode of industrial disputes resolution which is as sensitive to the associational interests of employees as the traditional strike/lock-out mechanism, it is not inconceivable that, some day, a system with fewer injurious incidental effects will be developed. In the meantime, in my view, legislatures are justified in abrogating the right to strike and substituting a fair arbitrating scheme, in circumstances when a strike or lock-out would be injurious to the economic interests of third parties. [22]

In this tortuous way, the Chief Justice's opinions sanctioned not only the regulation of the right to strike and collective bargaining of the kind that existed in the general legislation of the earlier era, but, as well, much of the "permanent exceptionalism" of the new era. To be sure, had the Court followed his judgement, it would have given a larger role to judicial review in the protection of freedom of association for workers; and by placing the onus on governments to demonstrate the validity of their actions under the terms of s. 1 of the Charter it would perhaps have served as a brake on governments. At the very least it would have institutionalized the potential for continuing juridical dissonance.

This would even more have been the case had the Court been persuaded by Justice Wilson's dissenting opinion; something, we may suspect, of which the Court was quite cognizant. Justice Wilson had concurred fully with the Chief Justice's dissent in the *Alberta Reference* case, against the majority ruling which had sanctioned the substantive denial of freedom of association to public and para-public employees *tout court*. But she was far more willing than Dickson in her dissent, to follow the logic of the defense of freedom of association to a judicial condemnation of "permanent exceptionalism" as well. Justice Wilson would not follow the Chief Justice in his equivocations over the constitutionality of the federal "6 and 5" legislation under s. 1 of the Charter. While she accepted that controlling inflation could have justified a limit, at the time on the general freedom of employees to bargain collectively and strike, she insisted that the actual legislation failed to meet the Court's own standard of not being "arbitrary, unfair or based on irrational considerations." The government had conceded that the controls on federal public employees were *not* expected to have a *direct* effect on inflation. The objective of persuading other workers to enter voluntarily into "6 and 5" agreements, using as example public sector controls, had clearly overstepped the bounds of what was permissable for government to do as an employer:

> ... the Canadian polity has rejected the notion that public sector collective bargaining and strike action threatens the sovereignty of the elected government. Instead we have allowed collective bargaining and strikes to play an important role in public sector labour relations. The rationale is clear; in most cases, it is eminently reasonable that the government bargain with someone from whom it wants to purchase a service. ... Prior to the enactment of the impugned legislation the government was demonstrating its leadership. The evidence clearly indicates that through the normal collective bargaining process the federal government had succeeded in keeping federal government settlements below the rate in the private sector and in the provincial public sectors. The government, however, was not satisfied. It wanted to use its role as legislator to make a dramatic gesture concerning its commitment to fighting inflation.... But in doing so it violated the fundamental rights of its employees under the Charter.... It seems somewhat paradoxical for the government to seek to inspire *voluntary* compliance by imposing a programme of *mandatory* compliance. One might well ask how this can be seen as setting an example of voluntary compliance by either government or its employees.
>
> The Chief Justice points to the restrictions placed on provincial government employees to show that the federal government's example was followed. I agree that the federal government's example was followed but it was the example of mandatory controls on the public sector. It was not demonstrated that the stated goal of inspiring voluntary compliance was achieved.... (T)he measures adopted were "arbitrary" and "unfair" in that they were imposed upon a captive constituency.... [23]

In her dissent on the *Dairy Workers* back-to-work legislation, Justice Wilson also pointed out that the Chief Justice had gone well beyond his acceptance of the ILO's definition of "essential services." His ruling could not rest, as she correctly pointed out, on the interruption of services which endangered "the life, personal safety or health" of even part of the population, but on the harm done to the economic interests of a "third party." It had not been established "that the provision of milk is an 'essential' service in the same sense that hospitals, fire-fighters, police and the like are providing essential services." And as for the "third party" in question, they were, in this case, the dairy farmers, many of whom were owners of the Dairy Producer's Co-operative, the largest employer involved in the dispute. "I have difficulty in appreciating how the owners of a corporation involved in the strike as a principal can be viewed as innocent third parties for purposes of assessing the harm suffered by such parties." Justice Wilson used her dissent in this case to reflect more broadly on one important dimension of what we have called "permanent exceptionalism":

> Past discussions as to when government should intervene to prohibit strikes has always focussed on the question of when it is *best* for government to intervene, not the question of when it is constitutional for it to do so ... I do not doubt that economic regulation is an important government function in today's society, but, if it is to be done at the expense of our fundamental freedoms, then it must, in my view, be done in response to a serious threat to the well-being of the body politic or a substantial segment of it. ...Legislatures in Canada have frequently intervened to prevent strikes in "essential services." Essential services initially comprised such things as public utilities, transportation and communications, but the legislative definitions have gradually broadened to cover firefighters and police and more recently the media, teachers and some classes of public employees.
>
> What conclusions are we to draw from this progressive expansion of the concept of "essential services"? Is this the route through which increasing government intervention in labour disputes is to be justified, namely that more and more goods are to be designated as "essential"?[24]

Justice Wilson's arguments, however compelling, were as little in synchrony with her fellow judges as they were with most of the Canadian political elite in the 1980s or the perspectives of the capitalist class proper. Her approach for rendering labour law juridically coherent in Canada, in the age of the Charter, was not on the cards. But neither can it be said that the Supreme Court's majority ruling just mirrored what legislatures had done or capitalists had demanded. The coherence the Court lent to labour law in the 1980s did indicate that law, as Engels put it, not only "reacts ... on the economic base," but that "it may, within certain limits modify it." This is usually taken to mean that it renders the economic base less subject to the norms of capitalist class domination and the untrammeled laws of accumulation. But this is *not* necessarily always the case. In spite of the claim made by Senator Eugene Forsey, immediately after the Supreme Court's decision, that "legally, this simply leaves things the way they were before the Charter was passed in 1982," [25] the Court had, in fact, gone well beyond sanctioning the regulation of free collective bargaining or even "permanent exceptionalism." Rather, by virtue of the breadth of its ruling that freedom of association did not constitutionally protect workers' rights to bargain collectively and strike *at all*, it juridically and ideologically provided space for a much broader assault on trade union freedoms no less in the private than the public sector.

To be sure, the first shots after the ruling were still fired at public sector workers. John Bullock, of the Canadian Federation of Independent Business, stated that his group would now be free to "pursue our own political action agenda to restrict the right to strike in the post office." At the same time, Roger Hamel, president of the Canadian Chamber of Commerce, announced his pleasure at the decision and used this occasion to reiterate his organization's demands for the elimination of strikes in "essential services." Even more significant, however, were the judgement's implications for the general collective bargaining regimes in most Canadian jurisdictions, in the context of the economic and political conditions of the 1980s. The ideological impact of the judgement was, in fact, immediate. As it happened, the Supreme Court ruling appeared only six days after reactionary new changes to the labour relations law were announced in British Columbia. The timing was, no doubt, largely coincidental, but it was used quickly by class warriors of Bullock's ilk to exult that the Supreme Court had shown the B.C. government's new assault on trade union freedoms, in the private as well as public sector, "would be legal." [26] The putative grounds for union court challenges to restrictive legislation had been undermined, within the context of what one eminent scholar of labour law discerned, in 1985, as the powerful emergence of "latent employer hostility to collective bargaining itself." [27]

The new era of coercion was given its juridical stamp of approval by the Supreme Court in 1987 in a manner more sweeping and authoritative than the era of free collective bargaining had been given its stamp by the 1946 Rand ruling. And yet, in the earlier era, some sectors and provinces had lagged behind, due to specific ideological and political, as well as economic, conditions; so too the way the new coercion manifested itself across Canadian society in the mid-to-late 1980s and beyond would depend on the economic as well as the ideological and political conditions in various parts of the country. At the same time—in so far as the Supreme Court's ruling meant that the legal framework of collective bargaining now provided a much less stable set of guarantees for union rights— the Supreme Court judgement could contribute paradoxically to the labour movement turning away from the legalistic practice in which it had become enveloped and renewing mobilization and politicization. It is important to bear all this in mind as we now examine further trends to a more generalized coercive regime in Canadian labour relations; the limits of reform in this context; and, finally, the labour movement's response.

CHAPTER 5

Consolidating a New Era of Coercion

The marked decline in the incidence of strikes and lockouts and the fact that over 90% of settlements are reached without a work stoppage are testimony to the inherent dynamism of the institution of free collective bargaining.

Professor P. Kumar [1]

For this so-called "rebirth of the trade union movement" to be genuine.... it would have to include independent unions administered and led by officials who were nominated freely and elected by secret ballot. They must also have the rights normally associated with labour unions, including the strike weapon.... The right to strike would technically exist.... but would be severely cramped by complex regulations.

The Globe and Mail [2]

If freedom of association only protects the joining together of persons for common purposes, but not the pursuit of the very activities for which the association was formed, then that freedom is indeed legalistic, ungenerous, indeed vapid.

Chief Justice Brian Dickson [3]

There were those in the labour movement, not least the president of the CLC, Dennis McDermott, who claimed at the time of the 1984 election that the turn to coercion was primarily attributable to the "obscene political immorality" of the Trudeau government. [4] From this perspective, the election of a new federal government, headed by the son of a skilled worker who, as opposed to the pretensions of a philosopher king, flaunted his experience in collective bargaining and his commitment never to cross a picket line, might have halted if not reversed the trend to coercion. After all, Mulroney presented himself as a pragmatic politician in the Mackenzie King mould (as opposed to an ideologue like Reagan or Thatcher) and shared King's background as a labour negotiator for monopoly capital. Indeed, Mulroney's *Economic Summit*, held shortly after his election, did appeal to the corporatist hopes of the CLC and QFL leadership. [5]

How ephemeral this was. If Canada has not experienced the same rise of neo-conservative ideology as Britain and the United States, it has hardly escaped the "strong state and free market" practice evidenced in those countries and elsewhere in the 1980s. This practice has included the continued routine of spying on peace groups, radical parties and trade unions; as well, it threatened civil liberties in such recent Conservative measures as the new anti-pornography legislation, the new immigration bill and the proposed new *Emergency Powers Act*. But integral to the strong state so necessary to create a "free" market, is the continuation and consolidation of the present assault on trade union rights and freedoms.

Whereas the Trudeau Government's central concern was to break the back of wage militancy in the context of double-digit inflation, the Mulroney Government's main concern was to attune the state more directly, and much more fundamentally, to the broader business agenda of the 1980s. The Trudeau Government's wage controls were not inconsistent with an enhanced regulatory role for the state in the economy generally, evidenced by the National Energy Programme and the expanded role for the Foreign Investment Review Agency. But the American state's and capital's reaction to these policies, overdetermined by the 1982 recession, put paid to this orientation. Since the late 1970s, the pace of capitalist restructuring at the level of the firm, and internationally, had been accelerating. It became clear that this had to entail, insofar as capital was concerned, extensive restructuring of the state itself, above all, a process of deregulation, privatization and the commodification of social services. It also entailed a restructuring of the labour process in the firm and the state, central to which was the extraction of significant concessions in the terms and conditions of employment entrenched in existing collective agreements. In this context, the Trudeau Government's freezing of collective agreements in the public sector was hardly sufficient.

We shall begin with an examination of the Mulroney Government's intrusions on labour's rights. Apart from attenuating the right to strike in the federal public sector, via the spurious designation of workers as "essential," the Mulroney Government directed the attack, above all, against those workers under federal jurisdiction who were most immediately affected by privatization and deregulation and, more generally, by the capitalist restructuring of industry in both public and private corporations. By overseeing elaborate strikebreaking schemes using scabs in Crown corporations, and by using back-to-work legislation of a particularly draconian kind (which intervened directly in the most basic aspects of freedom of association), the Mulroney Government carried this assault to unprecedented levels. In this way, the federal government has continued to provide an "example" for the private sector and provincial governments.

As we turn to examine developments in provincial jurisdictions, we shall see that most provincial governments hardly needed encouragement. Between 1985-87, there were no less than eighteen instances of suspensions of the right to strike via back-to-work measures at the provincial level. Taken with the federal measures, this amounted to an annual rate higher than in any previous period. (See Table III in Chapter II and Appendix I.) Generally, in the provinces, three broad lines of development can be discerned. First, the move toward permanent restrictions noted in Chapter Three in a number of provinces continued, and increasingly entailed the rewriting of labour codes to undermine workers' rights in the private as well as the public sectors. Secondly, permanent and direct interventions in the internal conduct of union affairs frequently became a central element in this process. And thirdly, as at the federal level, there was evidence of strengthening executive powers over labour at the expense of legislatures and public debate.

These developments have not occurred uniformly at the provincial level. They have been particularly, albeit not exclusively, evident in those provinces with governments having an explicitly neo-conservative ideology. But ideology alone is not a determinant. The uneven development of the Canadian economy produces uneven pressures on provincial governments. Provinces which are highly resource dependent have been severely squeezed through the 1980s, as falling international commodity prices and declining markets have rendered their economies more crisis-prone than others. The ensuing pressure to resolve the crisis at the cost of workers' rights is reinforced by the need to create a cheap and docile labour force, especially if they are to realize whatever hopes governments have of inducing capital into provincially-based strategies of economic diversification. In this regard, further restrictions on labour rights were prompted, not least, by workers' continuing refusal to stand idly by as rights so crucial to their dignity and material well-being were being suppressed.

It is our contention throughout this book that consent and coercion are not mutually exclusive phenomena. Just as the reforms of the previous era were enmeshed in a web of juridical restrictions, and just as the old era developed unevenly, it should not be surprising that instances of reform can be found in the new context. A parallel emphasis of this chapter, therefore, will be to examine the reforms introduced in the 1980s. The most significant, although it does not involve an extension of trade union rights, has been pay equity for women, in four provinces, discussion of which appears in the last section. Apart from this, the main exceptions to the continuing coercive trend are Manitoba and Ontario, whose present governments do not share the conservative ideological predispositions typical of the period. But, again, ideology alone does not determine the agenda. The political agenda of these governments has to be seen in the context of a robust economic recovery and falling rates of unemployment in these provinces. Seen in this context, the remarkable fact about the reforms coming from the more or less progressive governments in Ontario and Manitoba of the late 1980s, is how narrow they have really been. It brings into sharp relief the boundaries of reform in even the fairly positive conditions of two provinces.

The Mulroney Record

The Mulroney Government's initial approaches to consult the national union leadership paralleled the "Quality of Working Life" strategy of the capitalist firm, as a means for this restructuring. But it was doomed to failure, given the substance of what attuning the state to the free market entailed. The free market could not do without a strong state. The Mulroney Government's own resort to coercion in labour relations was virtually inevitable once bargaining was resumed in the wake of Trudeau's controls. It is also notable that centre stage was now given to a government strategy of securing concessions from those state workers who most stood in the way of capitalist restructuring and the privatization and deregulation that this entailed. These were the workers that always lay at the heart of the Canadian state's productive activities; who, in other words, provided the public infrastructure for private capital accumulation. This shifted state practice *vis-à-vis* strikes, and the terms of back-to-work legislation, in a direction that carried the assault on workers' trade union rights to unprecedented levels. The first example of this, the *Maintenance of Ports Operations Act* of November 1986, ended a lockout of dockworkers by B.C. maritime employers. The government imposed the concessions bargaining strategy of capital, and in so doing, went considerably beyond what had come before. Firstly, the government imposed a settlement based on a conciliator's report which included an absolute wage freeze for 1986, and increases for the next two years well below the expected rate of inflation. [6] At the same time, the primary cause of the dispute, the employers' demand for the elimination of a clause dating back to 1970 (governing the handling of "containers") from the collective agreement, was made subject to binding arbitration. With this, the government was signalling its preparedness (in more than one way, as we shall see) to play a new role, going well beyond wage restraint, in the capitalist restructuring characteristic of this era.

In early 1987, the Mulroney Government took up this strategy of concession bargaining directly, sweepingly applying it to employees of federal Crown corporations, and ultimately, using its powers of coercion to impose it unilaterally in most cases. By the spring of 1987, 100,000 workers in three federal industries (the seaway, railway and postal sectors) were facing similar demands by Crown corporations for concessions involving work rules, job security and wages. Informed observers saw the federal government actively pushing the unions concerned into taking strike action just to defend their current collective agreements. Even Bill Kelly, Labour Canada's omnipresent mediator, predicted "We have the makings of real trouble in some of the company demands ... It certainly could be a long hot summer." [7]

By the time the inevitable confrontations occurred, the government was well-armed with new back-to-work legislation, and more. It was hardly unprecedented for striking railway workers to be ordered back to work, as they were in the summer of 1987; most rail strikes since 1950 had been so dealt with. Arguably, the leaders of the railway unions had come to view such legislation as an avenue to arbitrated settlements yielding sufficient returns to get members off their backs. But with the 1987 back-to-work legislation (Bill C-85), the government was no longer prepared to play this game. The Bill pointedly ignored a conciliation report which had dismissed the railroads' key demands for the unfettered right to contract-out work and a two-tiered wage system. Furthermore, unlike the 1973 legislation ending the last rail strike, there was no provision for an interim wage settlement. Nor was there any stipulation that an arbitrator preserve existing job security provisions, let alone one stating that union concerns regarding the adequacy of these provisions be taken seriously. [8]

Given the resort to such onerous terms, it is not surprising that sanctions for disobeying the legislation escalated dramatically. In the case of Bill C-85, non - compliance was punishable by fines of $10,000-$50,000 per day for individual union officers and representatives, and $20,000-$100,000 per day for the union. Even individual members were subject to heavy fines of $500-$1,000 for non-compliance. [9] By contrast, the 1973 legislation had not set fines for non-compliance. Even if the government had little to fear from such a time-serving leadership, the reaction of the members could not be ignored. As the chief negotiator for the unions put it: "There's absolutely nothing in there for us ... Some [workers] may not want to obey it." [10] The ugly scene on this book's cover, of riot police in full gear on Parliament Hill arrayed against protesting railway workers, symbolizes the consequence of denying the fundamental freedoms that the Charter had so blithely promulgated. How ironic that the night before, Pierre Trudeau, whose government had beaten a path to this denouement, should have re-appeared before a parliamentary committee to ridicule Mulroney's Meech Lake Accord for violating the spirit of his Charter. Such is the character of Canada's political elite.

But, nowhere has Ottawa's willingness to transgress workers' rights been more clearly evident than in the case of Canada Post employees. Having earlier set a two-year deadline for eliminating Canada Post's deficit, and having staffed the corporation with aggressive managers brought in from the private sector, the government, urged on by the business community, was quite prepared to break the LCUC and CUPW's resistance to management's subsequent demands for massive concessions.[11]

For a Crown corporation to undertake, and the federal government to endorse, plans that involved mass-hiring of scabs and transporting them through picket lines in preparation for a strike, was a shocking departure from all modern experience. The use of private security agents to spy on pickets, including following them home once the strike began, added a particularly ugly dimension to the use of state coercion against workers. In the case of the letter carriers' strike in August 1987, these tactics, and the picket line violence they produced, yielded substantial popular revulsion (to which the media contributed by exposing the chaos initial use of these tactics created for the postal service). This caused the government to back off and support a negotiated settlement. However, both the government and Canada Post were determined that this would not happen with the inside workers. From the outset, the government's clear alternative for CUPW was capitulation or back-to-work legislation, even while it stepped up the strikebreaking tactics employed earlier. Despite CUPW's strategy—limiting disruption to rotating strikes and obvious efforts to minimize picket-line violence— in the face of Canada Post's provocative use of scab labour, back-to-work legislation (Bill C-86) came only eight days after the strike began.

To appreciate the government's extremism, it is necessary to review the issues involved in the strike. At the dispute's heart was job security: CUPW was essentially defending itself against management's efforts to reduce the workforce, not least, through its "franchising" programme which would contract-out some four thousand wicket positions. As day jobs, away from the noise and oppressive supervision of the large mail-sorting plants, these are perhaps the most desirable jobs available to CUPW members. Defending these positions, the union argued that Canada Post's plan would harm the community by extending the scope of casual and low-paid employment and changing the post office from a public service to that of a profit-maximizing business. Hundreds of thousands of workers in years past have bargained, and gone on strike, over similar issues.

To the government, the *issue* was the *union*. Consumer Minister Harvie Andre saw Bill C-86 as the only way to correct an intolerable situation in which "total excess labour cost ... is between $ 460 and 800 million a year. This situation exists not because the workers are lazy, but because of acquiescence to union demands. The present work rules are impossible." [12] The back-to-work legislation was designed, not merely to end the strike but to rectify this situation. In particular, the arbitrator was required in the original version of the Bill to take "due cognizance" of the conciliator's report released prior to the strike. This report, praised by Canada Post and the government, strongly supported Canada Post's franchise programme.

Finally, note that the possibility of a union as solidaristic and democratic as CUPW refusing to obey Bill C-86—despite massive financial penalties—brought to full public light just how far the assault on worker's rights had gone by the fall of 1987. Not only did Bill C-86 bar any union officer or representative (i.e. shop steward) convicted of violating the act from employment by Canada Post for five years, it also went on to ban any officer or representative so convicted from holding *any* union office for five years. This state suppression of the freedom of a private association's members to elect their own representatives, transgressed the most basic element of freedom of association. This, we have seen in the previous chapter, even the most conservative Supreme Court justices could not contemplate as possible in "democratic" Canada.

The publicity surrounding this dispute, and its draconian resolution, revealed that this was *not* just an *ad hoc* action directed at J.C. Parrot, in view of his previous defiance of back-to-work legislation, or even at CUPW, given its militant history. Consumer Minister Harvie André revealed that the Department of Labour was already routinely including such a clause in back-to-work legislation, having sought and obtained assurance as to its constitutionality from Department of Justice lawyers. [13] In fact, it didn't receive much attention at the time, but this same sanction for union non-compliance had actually been included in the *Maintenance of Ports Operations Act* a year earlier (notwithstanding the fact that the dispute was a lockout rather than a strike)—and a full six months in advance of the Supreme Court's supine decision extolling the virtues of Canadian democracy as against "totalitarianism."

The federal government's intolerance for substantive trade union rights has not been limited to back-to-work legislation. It can also be seen in its treatment of the efforts of Parliament Hill workers to organize. Taking advantage of the fact that these workers were not explicitly included under the purview of the PSSRA (or any other legislation), the PSAC, who had signed up a majority of these workers, obtained certification under the *Canadian Labour Relations Act*, rather than the more restrictive PSSRA. Unhappy with this "high-handed" affront to the sovereignty of parliament, the government appealed (ultimately successfully) the CLRB's decision to the federal court. Meanwhile, it passed Bill C-45, the *Parliamentary Employment and Staff Relations Act* in June 1986. This "gave" these workers limited collective bargaining rights, similar to those provided for by the PSSRA, but minus the right to strike—a right which, along with many other vital ones, they would have enjoyed under the CLRB certification.   For federal workers already certified under the PSSRA (which recognizes their right to strike), the government extended the use of its power, confirmed by the 1982 Supreme Court decision concerning air traffic controllers, to "designate" their work as "essential," thereby removing their right to strike. Table VI, which updates Table IV from Chapter III, compares the percentage of each bargaining unit "designated" before the 1982 Supreme Court decision with the percentage designated in the most recent round of bargaining. [14]

Table VI (page 74) clearly shows the legal right to strike for federal public sector workers exists mainly on paper. Almost 60 per cent of the bargaining units have more than one half of their members "designated." For the three largest bargaining units (CR, PM and GLT), who represent almost one-half of the PSAC membership, designations average almost 40 per cent. The only bargaining units to escape crippling designation levels are those which lack any meaningful bargaining power. That this power rather than any reasonable concept of "essentiality" governs designations is further reflected in the fact that in several cases, designation levels exceeded 100 per cent of the bargaining unit. Jobs, not workers, are designated, and some of these are so "essential" that the government hasn't even bothered to fill them!

This *de facto* intolerance of the trade union rights of organized workers is not confined to designations. Since the late 1970s, the PSAC has favoured unifying its many collective agreements with the federal government into one master agreement. No progress occurred in this direction until the mid-1980s, in part, because of a certain coolness toward the idea within PSAC leadership. However, the Mulroney Government was prepared to meet the union "half way," offering to negotiate one master agreement on non-monetary issues (i.e. technological change, job security, health and safety) but not on monetary issues, which would still be negotiated separately. This offer was conditional upon PSAC abandoning its right to strike over negotiation of the master agreement for "binding conciliation." The only thing surprising in all this is that the union leadership agreed, touching off a divisive internal struggle which ultimately forced the leadership to disavow "binding conciliation" in future negotiations.

The Mulroney Government's actions have led even centrist observers of labour relations at the federal level to suggest that the government's "longer range game plan appears to call for the gradual elimination of the strike option in federal dealings." [15] Further support for this contention is reflected in the government's proposed amendments to the PSSRA, unveiled in early 1987. These included new powers for the PSSRB, enabling it to delay strikes by appointing a conciliation officer, commissioner or board. Arguably more significant is the proposed expansion of the powers of the government as employer, empowering the Treasury Board to lay off and lock out employees (such as to vitiate any

TABLE VI
Percentage of Bargaining Units Designated as Essential—
Before and After the 1982 Supreme Court Decision [16]

Bargaining Unit	Percentage Designated before 1982	Percentage Designated 1987
Technical		
Air Traffic Control	10	100
Aircraft Operations	20	98
Drafting and Illustration	arb [a]	14
Education Support	arb	16
Electronics	27	69
Engineering and Scientific Support	14	33
General Technical	arb	60
Photography	arb	7
Primary Products Inspection	43	75
Radio Operations	55	arb
Ships' Officers	67	67
Social Science Support	arb	2
Technical Inspection	arb	66
Administrative Support		
Clerical and Regulatory	20	35
Communications	44	80
Data Processing	25	63
Office Equipment Operation	arb	19
Secretarial, Stenographic, Typing	arb	2
Operational		
Correction	111	111
Firefighters	arb	103
General Labour and Trades	21	63
General Services	31	80
Heat, Power and Stationary Plant Operations	64	105
Hospital Services	54	107
Lightkeepers	arb	106
Printing Operations Supervisory	arb	28
Printing Operations Non-Supervisory	27	21
Ships' Repair [b]	2	100
Ships' Crews	65	114

Scientific and Professional		
Defence Scientific Service	2	3
Engineering and Land Surveying	5	18
Library Science	0	0
Meteorology	58	92 [a]
Nursing	100	100
Occupational and Physical Therapy	21	100
Pharmacy	100	100
Physical Sciences	9	13
Psychology	76	100
Scientific Regulation	43	57
Scientific Research	3	na
Social Work	33	74
Veterinary Science	50	100
Administrative and Foreign Service		
Administrative Services	arb	14
Computer Systems Administration	9	8
Information Service	arb	2
Program Administration	arb	38
Purchasing and Supply	arb	68
Translation	12	13
Welfare Programs	arb	98

Sources: Information compiled from the public sector unions involved and the Public Service Staff Relations Board.

a. In response to its higher designation, the group switched to arbitration.

b. Groups negotiating under the arbitration process are not designated. Seven bargaining units that opted for arbitration before and after 1982 have not been included in the table. These groups are: Auditing, Commerce, Economics, Sociology and Statistics, Education, Financial Administration, Law and Medicine. Another 10 groups went from arbitration to binding conciliation but were never designated because there was a settlement. These bargaining units are: Actuarial Science, Agriculture, Architecture and Town Planning, Biology, Chemistry, Dentistry, Forestry, Historical Research, Home Economics, and Mathematics.

attempt by the PSAC to undertake coordinated strike action). More threatening is the proposed expansion of the definitions of "management" and "essential." As regards the former, the trade union rights of the whole PM group (the second largest unit with some twenty-four thousand members) could be expunged. As for the latter, according to PSAC President, Daryl Bean, this could mean an average level of designations across bargaining units of 80 per cent which "would destroy collective bargaining in the public service." [17]

The proposed changes to the PSSRA don't stop at further circumscribing the right to strike. As we shall see, in Quebec and British Columbia, the Treasury

Board also sought changes to the PSSRA institutionalizing wage controls within the collective bargaining process. By making the conciliation-strike route virtually unrealistic for PSAC members, the proposed changes would make arbitration more attractive as more issues would be opened to it. The "catch" is that arbitrators would be obliged to consider Ottawa's economic and fiscal policies when making awards. Already more conservative than wage settlements negotiated through the conciliation-strike route, arbitration would lower awards even further, [18] pushing public employees' wages far below those in the private sector.

Such an outcome is seemingly the central object of this entire reorganization of collective bargaining. As one observer concluded in a recent study of wage settlements in the Canadian public sector, "The debate on free-trade in Canada is already underway, and when free-trade becomes a reality in Canada, the requirement to be increasingly competitive in world markets will have one major policy implication for public sector compensation—namely that governments will pursue and apply even more vigorously a public policy that compensation levels in the public sector must follow and not lead the private sector." [19]

This conclusion is further underscored by the government's decision to suspend the fifty-year old practice of posting a minimum wage schedule for any federal construction project for three years, beginning April 1, 1987. Since the schedule corresponded closely to construction union collective agreements, this practice essentially secured unionized federal construction projects. Suspending this practice—leaving the market to set a fair wage, as Labour Minister Pierre Cadieux blithely put it—will open federal construction to cut-rate non-union contractors. [20] For the leaders of construction unions, who opted to leave the CLC rather than risk compromising their commitment to autocracy, and unbridled class collaboration, the government's announcement was a humiliating if well-deserved slap in the face.

We must conclude our discussion of increasing coercion under the Mulroney Government by pointing to its most disturbing aspect from the point of view of representative government in a liberal democracy. Included among the government's proposed amendments to the PSSRA is one empowering the cabinet to end strikes by Order in Council when Parliament is not in session. Thus, a strike allowed by parliamentary legislation, could be abrogated, not by act of legislature, as required by the rule of law in a parliamentary system (which is why we have back-to-work *legislation*), but by mere executive order. Moreover, the removal of such a fundamental freedom before had to be at least openly debated and passed through a representative assembly. This entailed broader public debate before arbitrary action is taken; with the proposed amendments, it now breaks upon the workers concerned from behind closed doors. In fact, this shift to increase executive power would neither be unprecedented nor confined to the federal level. The first moves in this direction came earlier in Alberta, New Brunswick and British Columbia (see Appendix I). As well, in the P.Q.'s amendments to the Quebec Labour Code in 1982, the government was enabled by Order in Council to suspend the right to strike where opinion held that public services designated as essential were not being sufficiently provided. [21] This procedure, as we shall see, is now being generalized to include the private sector in B.C. and Alberta.

Our argument has been that even before the controls period, the move toward routine back-to-work legislation undermined workers' right to strike. This, and its continuation through the 1980s, itself constituted a serious abridgement of fundamental freedoms. What we have just described reflects not only the further normalization of this practice, but also an attenuating democratic procedure at the state level. As is so often the case, this pruning of workers' fundamental freedoms tends to atrophy democratic processes within the state.

The Western Provinces

The consolidation of coercion at the provincial level, as the controls period came to an end, did not simply follow the federal lead, but in a number of cases broke new ground. Nowhere has this been more evident than in British Columbia. The deal Jack Munro struck at Kelowna with Bill Bennett, on behalf of the British Columbia Federation of Labour, proved to be anything but a durable truce, and came unstuck as soon as the Socreds—resurrected from an apparent deathbed by Bill Vander Zalm's smarmy smile—won re-election. The government's first priority, omitted from their electoral sales pitch, involved significantly extending the legislative assault begun earlier in the decade. Introduced, in the words of Labour Minister Lyall Hanson, "to increase our labour stability." [22] Bill 19, the *Industrial Relations Reform Act* (passed in June 1987), sought to secure the twin goals of "cost containment and international competitiveness" [23] for business by eroding further the organizational security of workers in the province.

This new legislation's severity is testament to the powerful economic and political forces pushing for a complete overhaul of the province's industrial relations. With union membership its lowest since 1947, and nominal wage increases at a virtual standstill—the result of continued high unemployment, public sector wage controls and the 1984 *Labour Code* revisions [24]—even the Business Council of B.C. conceded in 1985 that "There is a trend toward increases in wages and benefit costs being related to the profitability of individual firms and not to industry-wide, union-wide or national patterns or other external indices such as the consumer price index or inflation." [25]

Nonetheless, it was the renewed resistance of labour in B.C., symbolized by the IWA's successful seven-month strike against contracting-out [26] which set the stage for the new phase. Drafted behind the Labour Minister's back by private management lawyers, working under the auspices of the Premier's office, Bill 19 was described by the former Deputy Minister of Labour, Graham Leslie, as "the product of too few and too narrow minds...." [27] While employer representatives at first expressed concern over its radical interventionist aspects, they were pleased with the legislation's general thrust, which addressed many of their complaints about the 1973 Labour Code. By changing existing successor rights provisions, the definition of a related employer and rules regarding the rights of unions to include non-affiliation clauses in their agreements (forbidding contracting-out to non-union firms), this Bill promised to weaken enormously workers' power to prevent employers from escaping collective bargaining. [28] In the construction sector, Graham Leslie has suggested that Bill 19 could lead to total de-unionization.

Most striking is its unprecedented level of state intervention restricting union powers. Through the instrument of an Industrial Relations Council (IRC), chaired by a government-appointed commissioner, the government, for the first time, will wield the power to declare workers in the private as well as public sector "essential." If the Labour Minister "considers that the dispute poses a threat to the economy of the Province or to the health, safety or welfare of its residents or to the provision of education services," the Minister may order a forty-day cooling-off period and/or direct the IRC to "designate" any number of workers it considers necessary to ensure the provision of "essential" services. Failure to respect a back-to-work order constitutes "just and reasonable cause" for disciplinary action (i.e. dismissal) by the employer, and a new provision requiring the IRC to file its orders in the Supreme Court of British Columbia, upon request, aims to guarantee further union compliance.

This legislation lays the basis for massive interference, by the state and capital, in the freedom of unions to conduct their own affairs: the Industrial Relations Commissioner can order a vote during a strike or lockout on an employer's last offer; unions are prohibited from holding strike votes until they have bargained collectively in accordance with the act; and, employers can require workers to vote on the final offer prior to the commencement of a strike or lockout. Combined with provisions giving the employer "freedom to express his views provided he does not use intimidation, coercion or threats," such clauses patently intrude on workers' freedom of association. At the same time, workers' strike powers and rank-and-file solidarity are severely weakened by the IRC's power to prohibit secondary boycott agreements and restrict picketing "in such a manner that it affects only the operation of an employer causing the lockout or whose employees are lawfully on strike, or an operation of an ally of that employer."

The Commissioner is further empowered to refer any dispute to a mediation officer, "fact finder" or "public interest inquiry board." In the last case, the Commissioner "may at his discretion direct that a vote be conducted on the acceptance or rejection of the recommendations" of the board by the membership. Refusal to participate in the board's activities results in the preparation of an agreement by the other party.

As if all of the above were not sufficient, the cards are further stacked in favour of the employer by the requirement—stated no less than *seven* times throughout the *Act*—that any imposed first agreement, fact finder's report, public-interest inquiry board recommendations or binding arbitration involving a public-sector employer, must include due consideration of "ability to pay" criteria. This is defined broadly as "the current ability of a public sector employer to pay based on existing revenues, requirements of any fiscal policies to which the public sector employer is subject, and the impact of increased costs on the maintenance of existing levels of public service." The incorporation of these criteria into all aspects of public-sector bargaining under the *Act* thus extends the worse features of the *Compensation Stabilization Amendment Act* of 1983, by granting the new Industrial Relations Commissioner the power to overturn settlements without appeal. The fact that the original legislation was condemned by the ILO in 1986, as being "contrary to the principle of voluntary collective bargaining," [29] obviously made no impression on the drafters of Bill 19. Finally, this Bill contains three clauses which, while incorporated into the *Act*, have not been officially proclaimed. These clauses allow the government, or cabinet when the Legislative Assembly is not in session, to end any dispute and appoint a "special mediator" whose recommendations would constitute a binding agreement. While suspension of these clauses was presented by the government as an expression of good faith, the B.C. Federation of labour dismissed the move, noting that the Premier could "call a cabinet meeting and proclaim those sections in ten minutes." [30]

Charging that the new labour bill still contains clauses sufficient to weaken and even destroy unions, particularly in the construction industry, the BCFL pledged to boycott the Industrial Relations Council. The labour movement's reaction to Bill 19 appears justified in light of subsequent events. Even before passage, independent observers in the province pointed to the fundamentally anti-union thrust of the legislation. James Dorsey, secretary of the Arbitrators' Association of British Columbia, for example, noted that the "bill clearly encourages a non-union economy." [31] Short of the outright threat of de-unionization, the new Act promises to effect an increasing degree of self-imposed restraint on the unions. In their efforts to avoid the intervention of the IRC, for example, unions have attempted to secure agreements without resorting to job action. In the words of the chief negotiator for B.C. Rail, "The fact that the IRC sits there, with its awesome powers ... gives a catalyst to the parties to go head to head, trying at all costs to avoid a third party. I can see that in a very positive way." [32]

Bill 19 was accompanied by another piece of legislation, for teachers, presented as a measure granting them broader collective bargaining rights, including the long-sought right to strike. However, *The Teaching Profession Act* (Bill 20), in fact, weakens the power of one of the Government's most active opponents. In view of the new *Industrial Relations Act*'s severe restrictions on any job action which could be construed as threatening the "provision of educational services," the legal recognition of teachers' right to strike in Bill 20, must be seen as fundamentally meaningless. At the same time, Bill 19's overriding requirement that all public sector agreements meet "ability to pay" criteria, effectively blocks real negotiations over teachers' wages and benefit levels. Most important from the perspective of freedom of association, is the restructuring of the teachers' federation. Bill 20 separates teachers' bargaining and professional roles, weakening their ability to act collectively. The price of obtaining the right to strike was the fragmentation of the BCTF as a union. For those teachers who elect to organize as a union, the new BCTF will be broken up into separate local bargaining units— one for each school district. Those districts choosing not to re -enter the BCTF, or to stand alone as an independent union, will be subject to interest arbitration awards which must comply with the criteria set out in the *Industrial Relations Act*. Principals and vice-principals are expressly excluded from membership in the BCTF, their tasks defined in strictly managerial terms, and their duty to represent the school board on matters of educational policy reinforced by the board's absolute control over their terms of employment.

While the bargaining strength of teachers is fragmented and divided against itself, a new College of Teachers, which includes principals, vice-principals, superintendents and private school teachers as well as public school teachers, reinforces the government's control over teachers' professional activity. With one-quarter of the College's governing council holding office at the pleasure of the Cabinet, the college's responsibility to establish and enforce educational and profession standards, with "regard to the public interest" will be heavily influenced by government policy. As the BCTF has noted, the "college is a government agency rather than a representative body for teachers. It carries out functions now carried out by the Ministry of Education, and it is empowered to tax teachers for the cost of its activities." [33]

As with Bill 19, there has been a strong reaction against Bill 20. Within two weeks of the Bill's tabling in the B.C. legislature, the BCTF received a 70 per cent vote in favour of job action—the largest in its history. Following passage of the Bill, teachers participated in a one-day walkout called by the BCFL. In the words of Elsie McMurphy, president of the teachers' federation, "We are now a trade union; the government has made the decision." [34] While initial support for unionization under the BCTF has been good, there are organized factions, such as the Vancouver Teachers for Association, campaigning actively against the right to strike. Arlene Cook, secretary of VTA, commented that "We're opposed to teachers going out on strike ... and we've felt for a long time that the political causes and the social programs of the BCTF have not helped the education of children in this province." [35] Recently, the Minister of Education, Anthony Brummet, ordered school districts to release teacher lists to opposition organizations such as VTA in order to assist their membership drives against the BCTF.

In Alberta, a pattern similar to that of B.C. can be seen, although it developed somewhat more circuitously. The collapse of energy prices in the early- to mid-1980s reinforced the trend toward intensifying and generalizing the assault on trade union rights already underway. But this was, at the same time, a response to the determined resistance by Alberta workers, made even more remarkable by the province's reputation, over the past half-century, for its allegedly monolithic right-wing populism.

That important changes in popular consciousness were underway in Alberta was demonstrated during the violent six-month strike at the Gainer's meatpacking plant in 1986. The workers successfully defeated the attempt by the well-known right-wing entrepreneur and sometime Tory party activist, Peter Pocklington, to break their union. Canadians were shocked with the nightly display on national television of workers being injured, as armoured busloads of scabs, aided by the unprecedented use of Edmonton's riot squad, bulled their way through picket lines. These scenes helped produce widespread support for the strike—and for the picket line which continued, despite more than five hundred arrests in the first month alone. One labour historian drew a parallel to the 1919 Winnipeg General Strike, in terms of the impact of the Gainer's strike on people's thinking. [36] Over eight thousand Albertans marshalled at the provincial legislature to demand reforms protecting workers' rights. Even the NDP experienced a marked increase in votes and seats (especially around Edmonton) in the May 1986 provincial election.

In the face of this rebuke, and confronted by the threat of continued labour unrest, the newly-elected premier, Don Getty, agreed to a formal review of the province's labour legislation. But the Review Committee's Report completely evaded issues of key concern to the unions. Instead, the Committee sought major changes to collective bargaining, aimed at increasing government intervention, while further restricting workers' use of the strike weapon. The government's proposed revisions to the province's *Labour Code*, Bill 60, fully reflect these objectives. The government assumes enormous powers to intervene in collective bargaining on behalf of business—powers which embody a dramatic and qualitative shift in the role of the Executive *vis-à-vis* the right to strike.

Provisions similar to those as yet unproclaimed in B.C. are front and centre in the Alberta legislation in even more disturbing form. Bill 60 will enable the cabinet to end any dispute in which "damage to health or property is caused or is likely to be caused" as a result of a reduction in municipal or health services, or in any case where "unreasonable hardship" may result to a third party. Other changes include provisions forcing unions to hold votes on an employer's "final" offer and/or the recommendations of a mediator, and harsh sanctions for union non-compliance with mediation. Even when workers choose to strike under these onerous conditions, they must provide seventy-two hours notice of the location of such action and restrict picketing to members of the union concerned. Overall, the proposed *Labour Code* will have profoundly negative consequences for workers in Alberta. Not only does it increase the degree of arbitrary government intervention, delaying and even ending strikes without reference to the legislature, the new provisions allow the government and employers greater access to union members around the heads of their elected leadership, threatening to undermine the worker solidarity essential to successful bargaining. In combination with conspicuous silence on the issue of replacement workers (scabs), clauses restrict picketing and secondary boycotts, further weakening organized labour's capacity to oppose employers' demands at the bargaining table through the use of a credible strike threat. Finally, the failure to limit employers' right to restructure their activities to escape unions altogether, also reflects the Bill's pre-eminent focus: the enhancement of capital's flexibility to respond to a "competitive world economy," dutifully acknowledged in the preamble.

It is important to emphasize that the new labour code is not an attempt by the state to simply do away with unions and collective bargaining. Rather, it normalizes state intervention within a collective bargaining framework, in a manner that systematically shifts the balance of power toward capital. Thus, even in the construction industry, where de-unionization has proceeded space, amidst the near disappearance of collective agreements, the government passed a bridging act. Bill 53, on the same day that the new *Labour Code* was introduced (and scheduled to expire upon the new *Code's* passage) which provided a temporary collective bargaining framework for the industry. However, the Act not only accommodates employer demands for the elimination of sequential strikes and leapfrogging, by requiring centralized negotiations, but also imposes a two-year moratorium on grievances related to existing non-union "spin-off" firms, apparently introduced to allow those contractors to evade future collective agreements. It is worth noting that the absence of any provision in the proposed *Labour Code* concerning accreditation in the construction industry also suggests that the government is not prepared to restrict the freedom of employers to deal with workers in any way they desire. Furthermore, the collective bargaining envisioned is hardly "free." General conditions of employment are to be negotiated between ministerially designed "federations" and contractors and unions, with agreements lasting five years; and with the minister empowered to end any strike or lockout.

The restrictive new *Code* was introduced despite the harsh criticism of Alberta by the ILO mission to Canada, which declared that the restrictions on public sector workers' right to strike imposed by Bill 44 "go beyond acceptable limits which are recognized in Convention No. 87." [37] The Alberta government's contempt for this ruling was shown in its refusal to offer any improvements to the legislation governing state employees. Indeed, a 1985 amendment to the *Public Service Employee Relations Act* (Bill 30) actually broadened the power of the Public Service Employee Relations Board to exclude persons from a bargaining unit. Moreover, under the terms of the proposed *Code*, the same restrictions on arbitration board rulings imposed under Bill 44 will continue to apply. Any board will have to consider "any fiscal policies that may be declared from time to time in writing by the Provincial Treasurer," as well as "the need to maintain appropriate relationships in terms and conditions of employment between different classification levels within an occupation and between occupations in the employer's employment."

The structural erosion of workers' collective rights *within* the post-controls collective bargaining system is clearly evidenced in Saskatchewan, which, as we noted in Chapter III, was the first province to revise its *Labour Code* along the lines of the new era. Here, the legislation passed in 1983 has already worked to undermine the integrity of existing bargaining units while allowing employers, particularly in the construction industry, to operate free of unions entirely. Under Bill 24, governing the construction sector, an estimated 85 per cent of the work was being performed at non-union rates by 1986. [38]

The Labour Relations Board—especially under the chairmanship of Dennis Ball, a lawyer with strong Tory links—has played a key role in re-structuring the industrial relations system to the benefit of employers. The Board's interpretation of Bill 104's provisions on job status have led to the exclusion of ninety-five of ninety-seven liquor board employees from a union, while a subsequent decision resulted in twenty nurses being denied the right to belong to their union. [39] A January 1986 LRB decision, dismissing an unfair labour practices charge against Safeway, effectively opened the door for management to alter unilaterally its workers' terms of employment by overturning the accepted interpretation of the *Trade Union Act*'s bridging clause. [40] Subsequent protests by organized labour resulted in the government tabling Bill 8, *An Amendment to the Trade Union Act*, requiring an employer to establish bad faith on the part of a union before imposing its own contract terms. This Bill, however, was never passed into law. In early 1986, a Bill that *was* passed ended a strike by twelve thousand public employees. Imposing an agreement based on a previous conciliation report, and including a provision allowing for the dismissal of anyone disobeying the back-to-work order, the *SGEU Dispute Settlement Act* (Bill 144) contained the infamous clause we referred to in the previous chapter, exempting it from section 2(d)— "freedom of association"—of the *Charter of Rights and Freedoms*, as well as from similar provisions in the Saskatchewan Human Rights Code. As we noted, the government's invocation of the Charter's "notwithstanding" clause was a response to a decision by the Saskatchewan Court of Appeal ruling unconstitutional the back-to-work legislation passed in 1983-84. This immediately produced a furor among human rights groups across the country, although it hardly troubled the majority of Supreme Court justices themselves.

The marked deterioration of industrial jurisprudence in the province has been accompanied by what Bob Sass recently described as "a complete loss of confidence" by unions in the Department of Labour. Since May 1982, Sass note, eighty-four cases have gone to the minister for appointment of an arbitrator, with the union winning a total of four and losing nineteen; the rest were withdrawn "because of the unions' perception of an anti-union bias." [41] To add insult to injury, in its 1986 Throne Speech, the government announced a change of name for the Department of Labour. Consistent with its own business approach to workers, the department was now to be called the Department of Human Resources, Labour and Employment.

Quebec

The trend toward permanent, rather than temporary, legislation eliminating trade union rights was also evident in Quebec. In 1985, the P.Q. government followed the welter of "temporary" restrictions, imposed on workers in the public and para-public sectors during the controls period, with Bill 37, a complex Act which included amendments to the province's *Labour Code*, institutionalizing and extending these restrictions. The government's powers to restrict the extent of work stoppages were broadened significantly; its control over the actual content of any agreement in the area of monetary issues became almost absolute; further, as in Alberta, Bill 37 provided for a fundamental restructuring of the collective bargaining relationship.

With the public and para-public sectors, Bill 37 designates as "essential" anywhere from 55 per cent of workers in the social services to 90 per cent in special health-care centres. Exact numbers in any specific situation are to be negotiated by the union and the Essential Services Council; however, the Council may increase or modify required levels of service "if the situation of the establishment justifies it." Under the Act, bargaining is split into two levels, with monetary issues determined at the national level while most other job conditions are subject to local negotiations. At the national level, wage and salary scales are not subject to mediation, nor can the parties be bound to any recommendations. Work stoppages during the second or third year of a national level agreement, or with respect to matters negotiated at the local or regional level, are prohibited absolutely. In fact, the state enjoys the power to set wages and salaries during the last two years of an agreement. Following the publication of an annual report on remuneration in Quebec by a "neutral" pay research institute, the Treasury Board, in collaboration with management committees, "negotiate" with the unions on wage levels for the coming years. While in no case may the new levels be lower than those of preceding years, there is no provision in the law for arbitration, in the event that a voluntary agreement cannot be reached. Bill 37 simply states that the president of the Treasury shall table annually, in March, "a draft regulation fixing the salaries and salary scales for the current year," and that these shall subsequently form part of the existing collective agreement. [42]

At the same time that Bill 37 weakens the unions through severe restrictions on their right to strike, it hobbles their efforts at concerted bargaining by splitting negotiations into numerous sub-divisions. Not only are issues concerning job conditions relegated to local and regional negotiations, but unions are now required to conduct talks at the national level through a number of sectoral and sub-sectoral "tables." Thus, workers in the educational sector are divided according to teaching, non-teaching professional and support staff, while those in the social affairs sector are further split into five different divisions—social services, hospitals, reception centres, local community-service centres, and private hospital and reception centres. Each sectoral "sub-table" has complete discretion in determining if an article is discussed in whole or part, at either the "sub-table" or the sectoral table. [43] Finally, Bill 37, while splitting the unions, provides the Treasury Board with an overseeing role in national level negotiations, granting it the power to "authorize the bargaining mandates of the management committees and sub-committees in those matters that it considers to be of governmental interest."

The consequences of this reorganization of bargaining structures has been significant. The last round of wage talks were the first since 1972 in which the three largest public-sector groups were unable to form a Common Front. Undoubtedly, this failure was due, in large part, to tensions among the three federations, stemming from the refusal of the CNTU and QFL to back the CEQ's demand to restore wage levels eroded under the 1982 restraint legislation. However, by allowing the government to avoid negotiating at a central table, the new bargaining framework exacerbated existing divisions within union ranks. When the CNTU health workers, reeling from harsh back-to-work legislation, accepted a settlement in mid-December, "the pattern was set and dominos began falling." [44] This demonstrates how the Liberal government which succeeded the P.Q. has been able to make ready use of the inheritance bequeathed to it.

On its own bat, the Liberal government introduced in 1986 alone no less than six back-to-work measures, two of which were actually Orders-in-Council, removing the right to strike from particular groups of workers. The harshest legislation, passed in November 1986, ended a rotating strike by Quebec nurses. Described by one union representative as "the most severe law Quebec has had in the last twenty years," [45] Bill 160 not only permitted health organizations to hire strike breakers, but also allowed patients to lodge class-action suits for damages against the union. This remarkable degree of arbitrary state intervention against workers must be seen not simply as a reflection of the more "politicized" nature of labour relations in Quebec, but also as the consequence of changes to the Labour Code since 1982, which facilitate such interventions. In granting the Essential Services Council power to order individuals or groups of workers back to work, Bill 37 (as with Bill 19 in B.C. and Bill 61 in Alberta) takes this process one step further, forcing unions to confront a state apparatus ever more able, and willing to intervene in a dispute it deems threatening to the "public interest."

As witnessed in Western Canada, Quebec has, as yet, not moved toward restructuring the labour relations regime in the private sector. Two sharply divergent reports, both commissioned by the government, were released in 1986. The Beaudry Commission report, entitled *Work, a Collective Responsibility*, oriented toward facilitating union certification and improved workers' rights, was denounced by business as little more than a "union manifesto." [46] The second report, by a task force headed by Reed Scowan, parliamentary assistant to Premier Bourassa, took the theme "Regulate Less, Regulate Better." It presented proposals for, among other things: relaxation of the province's anti-scab laws; making the Health and Safety Commission's standards "more flexible;" the elimination of rigid rules governing hiring in the construction industry; and, amendments to the *Labour Code* to facilitate contracting out for "valid economic reasons." It was attacked by labour as "a declaration of war." [47] While it is not yet certain in which direction the government will move, its passage of Bill 119 abolishing the classification certificate, which controls access of workers to the construction industry, may well signal the direction of the Scowan Report is the one it intends to follow.

The Atlantic Provinces

In Atlantic Canada, the severe restrictions on trade union rights characteristic of the whole post-war era were exacerbated in that region by the wage restraint measures introduced under the wing of Trudeau's controls, and also by the new, permanent restrictions of Newfoundland's Bill 59. This led to widespread dissatisfaction among the trade unionists there who increasingly demanded fundamental reforms. This forms an indispensible context for examining developments in these provinces in the mid-1980s.

In New Brunswick, the fact that the Labour Relations Board is still a part-time operation illustrates the backwardness of the province's existing labour legislation. The absence of *any* progress in reforming labour legislation since 1981, led the provincial federation of labour, in May 1985, to vote unanimously to cease all further participation in the government's Industrial Relations Council. [48] This seems to have provoked the government to address partially the labour movement's demand for pay equity legislation by amending the *Employment Standards Act* (Bill 28), in June 1986. But labour's call for a full-time Labour Relations Board, let alone its calls for first-agreement legislation, limitations on "designations" and anti-scab legislation like Quebec's, remains unheeded.

In Nova Scotia, the only major legislative change in the post-controls period was regressive. Introduced in 1986, Bill 91 paralleled the restrictions imposed on private sector construction workers in the West. It required a vote on the employer's final offer before a strike could be called and narrowed permissible strike tactics to minimize the possibility of "leap frogging"—while imposing no limits on employers' ability to establish non-union spin-off firms. As one contractor said of the Act: "We consider it a very important piece of legislation ... Obviously, it plays a big role in all our negotiations now. We've come a long way from Marc Lalonde's letter asking what we were doing giving away $8.50 over four years in 1983." [49]

Developments in P.E.I., under the newly elected Liberal government led by Joe Ghiz, were more progressive. Following a Labour Relations Board decision, in the fall of 1985, which stated that employers were under no obligation to rehire striking employees, Ghiz pledged his party's support for reforms. After some delay, Premier Ghiz's government did make good on this promise by passing an amendment (Bill 55) to *The Labour Act*, in May 1987. This Bill, guaranteeing the reinstatement of any striking employees following the termination of job action, and the immediate layoff of any replacement workers, essentially did no more than restore the 1985 *status quo*. Bill 55 was also accompanied by another amendment to the *Labour Act*, Bill 47, which extended collective bargaining rights to nurses, hospital employees and non-instructional school personnel. However, these rights did *not* include the right to strike—a right enjoyed by many of their counterparts (school personnel especially) in other provinces—but rather, imposed binding arbitration as the ultimate dispute resolving mechanism. Finally, the government introduced a *Pay Equity Act* (Bill 75), not yet passed, covering the civil service, various Crown agencies, hospitals and nursing homes.

But by far the most important developments in Atlantic Canada took place in Newfoundland, where an illegal strike against Bill 59 by the Newfoundland Association of Public Employees (NAPE) constituted the most serious labour conflict in the Maritimes since the 1970 Canso strike in Nova Scotia. The context for this strike was set in April 1983, when the Newfoundland legislature debated and passed—in nineteen minutes—Bill 59, which, among other things, required public sector unions to designate up to 49 per cent of their members "essential," and thereby ineligible to strike.

Bill 59 merely added to the growing pressure for long overdue reform. The existing labour relations regime was such that no legislative changes were needed, as in the West, for 60-90 per cent of the construction industry to go non-union in the 1980s, through the incorporation of new "general contracting companies" to evade unionized workers.[50] Moreover, a Labour Standards Tribunal ruled that a majority of Newfoundland companies owed almost $100 million in back wages for ignoring from 1978 the required notice period regarding layoffs. This led to the perverse consequence of the government promptly exempting them by special retroactive legislation, forced through by closure. Justifying the government's action, the Labour Minister stated that "Nobody in his right mind wants to make legislation retroactive. Anyone with a sense of fairness wouldn't want to do it, but there was no other way. Either the companies paid, in which case a lot of them would have gone bankrupt, or government paid, and we went bankrupt. Neither of these were in the public interest." The president of the Newfoundland Teachers' Federation responded that "This legislation is the last message that has finally convinced people that Peckford has lost his vision for the common man and has succumbed to the interests of the traditional power brokers in Newfoundland—the large corporations."[51]

The 1985 provincial election saw the Conservative government suffer a significant setback. A key role in this was played by groups such as the Fishermen's Union, the Status of Women Council and the Roman Catholic Social Action Commission, organized under the banner of the pro-NDP "Coalition for Equality." In a bid to repair some of the damage, the Peckford government set up an inquiry into labour relations in the construction industry, and passed legislation (Bill 14) in June 1985, amending the province's *Labour Relations Act* to provide for compulsory dues check-off, and for the imposition of a first (collective) agreement. The first of these provisions is further testimony to how limited the existing legislation actually was. As for the second, labour's support notwithstanding, experience in other jurisdictions increasingly suggests this legislation is a poor antidote for bargaining unit weakness, with imposed first agreements, as often as not, being a step on the road to decertification rather than toward a "mature" bargaining relationship.[52]

In any event, these severely limited reforms did not touch Bill 59. NAPE's response to this legislation had been delayed by the two-year wage freeze imposed by the Peckford government during the controls period. However, as early as October 1984, its president, Fraser March signalled to his members that he was prepared to go to jail to defend their rights.[53] This courageous stand, implicitly endorsed by the ILO's ruling condemning Bill 59, may have encouraged the union, as it voted by 86 per cent to strike—without meeting the Bill's requirement of first designating essential workers—over the issue of achieving wage parity with other public sector workers.

Following the collapse of negotiations, twelve hundred NAPE members struck illegally. The government responded by applying for, and receiving, an injunction against the strike, accompanied by further threats of fines and suspensions. Attorney General Lynn Verge announced an investigation "into potential violations of provincial statutes and the Criminal Code" by NAPE leader Fraser March." There were mass arrests of picketers outside the Newfoundland legislature, including March and NDP leader Peter Fenwick.

These government actions mainly strengthened popular support for the union. In the context of the government's preoccupation with the strike's illegality and the restrictive labour legislation imposed by Canadian governments generally, the strike had become a struggle of great national significance. Two weeks after its start, over five thousand workers were on the picket lines. The Chief Justice of Newfoundland extended the injunction indefinitely, saying the situation in Newfoundland was approaching "anarchy." However, no further arrests were made due to fears that the arrest of hundreds, or even thousands, of strikers would clog the justice system.

After a month, the government relented and signed a "Memorandum of Understanding." In exchange for an end to the strike, the government declared its willingness to act on the union's demands for parity and amendments to Bill 59 which would grant all workers equal collective bargaining rights, including the right to strike. Negotiations then resumed, but little progress was made. The Treasury Board, unhappy with some of the provisions of the memorandum signed in the spring, was stonewalling progress.[54] In September, a second walkout took place, that was ended with the help of the churches' intercession. NAPE finally achieved its demand for parity—to be realized over three years. The issue of Bill 59 was another matter. Premier Peckford announced that while his government would agree to amend the Bill to make it "work better," it had no intention of repealing the legislation. "We can't allow one group to usurp the rule of law and everything most of us have come to respect ... We don't intend to move."[55] Two and one-half years later, his government still hasn't moved. Meanwhile, Fraser March joined the growing list of trade union leaders jailed by the Canadian state since 1972. He was sentenced to four months (NDP leader James Fenwick was jailed for two months as well), and placed on two years probation, and the union was fined $110,000. In its defence, the union argued that Bill 59 violated freedom of association and freedom of speech. Here we see the relevance of *The Globe and Mail* quotation at the outset of this chapter, asserting that any "genuine" trade union movement "must have the rights normally associated with labour unions, including the right to strike" which cannot just "technically exist." Thus, the union's view is shared by the prime organ of Canadian establishment opinion. In point of fact, the editorial was written some four years earlier, and was not about Canada at all, but about Poland. The fact that it could apply to Canada points to the limits of Canadian democracy in the 1980s. Indeed, speaking in his own defence, Fraser March alluded precisely to this: "Just take a look at what happened to Lech Walesa in Communist Poland and take a look at what happened to Fraser March in Democratic Canada ... I think that would tell you something of the problems that trade unions have in trying to represent their members."[56]

Manitoba and Ontario

It would be easy to be cynical about the meaning of reform in this new era of coercion, in light of events in Atlantic Canada. But arguably, Manitoba and Ontario, where more progressive governments have come to office in economic circumstances more congenial to reform, represent quite a different kettle of fish. Even in these cases, the limits of reform in this era are clearly visible.

In Manitoba, the NDP government introduced a number of significant reform measures. During the controls period, as noted in Chapter III, the *Labour Relations Act* was significantly amended (by Bill 22), which came into effect on January 1, 1985. In addition to revamping the Labour Board, simplifying and expediting the grievance-arbitration process, the amendments made unionizing easier and extended the legal protections afforded strikers. In particular, the use of "professional" strike breakers was proscribed and striking workers' right to reinstatement after the conclusion of a dispute was reinforced. The *Pay Equity Act* (Bill 53) was passed in 1985, and the government also amended the *Employment Standards Act* (Bill 74) that same year, providing paternity leave and increased notice in the case of mass layoffs. Finally, in 1987, the government passed Bill 61, amending the *Labour Relations Act* to allow for a form of binding arbitration known as "final offer selection."

What at first glance looks like a glowing record, not least in comparison with what has gone on in other jurisdictions, loses much of its shine upon closer inspection. Read from the perspective of reform, most striking about Bill 22 is its modesty. The amendments relating to certification, when compared to Federal or even Ontario provisions *prior* to the defeat of the Conservative regime, can hardly be said to break new ground. Similarly, the prohibition on the use of strike breakers fails to go beyond that enacted by the Davis government in Ontario let alone approaches the anti-scab legislation of the 1970s in Quebec during the P.Q.'s radical phase. Since the demand for professional strike breakers, given the supply of non-professionals and the practicality of their use in any form, is limited to quite specific circumstances, even an ardent defender of the NDP's reforms conceded that "perhaps 5 per cent, maybe 10 per cent, of all paid workers in the province would be affected or influenced by these provisions...."[57]

However, modesty is not the only aspect of Bill 22 revealed by critical examination of its contents. Several of its provisions, resembling developments characteristic of the new coercion, broaden the powers of government to intervene in collective bargaining and the internal affairs of unions. Included amendments imposed a duty of "fair representation" on unions; imposed new voting requirements for strikes and contract settlements; empowered the Labour Minister to appoint a mediator without the consent of the union; and, mandatorily included in a collective agreement, ongoing consultation upon the request of *either* party.[58]

This aspect of the Manitoba record becomes even more pronounced when considering the 1987 amendment to the Labour Relations Act (Bill 61) that allows for "final offer selection" (FOS). FOS is a form of binding arbitration where management and the union each present a "final" proposal to an arbitrator/selector, who chooses one of them to be the new collective agreement. It first surfaced in Manitoba (it already exists elsewhere, including Ontario, in slightly amended form) in 1984 as one of the NDP's proposed revisions to the Labour Code, but was omitted from Bill 22 when it proved to be controversial. Later reintroduced as a means for expanding the options available for avoiding work stoppages *via* Bill 61, it was pushed through the legislature over strong public opposition, not only by business groups but also, notably, by a significant segment of the labour movement.[59] Under the new legislation, (which is "experimental," i.e. it expires after five years unless renewed) FOS is made available to either party at specific points in negotiations, but requires approval by a majority of the members of the bargaining unit in order to be implemented.

The best that can be said of Bill 61 is that it could be used by a union local to pre-empt a lock-out by their employer, thereby saving a weak bargaining unit from a potentially fatal confrontation. This, apparently, was the basis of business' opposition to the Bill.[60] Looked at from another angle, Bill 61 may actually be seen as a step in the direction of developments in the other Western provinces: the NDP wrote into the Act the same kind of new arbitration requirements as in those provinces' restrictive legislation, notably that FOS selectors must take into account: "the employer's ability to pay" in making their choice. Secondly, it gives *employers* the right to demand a vote by workers; thus, allowing employers to sidestep union representatives. This is a dangerous precedent that a future conservative government could use to justify further intrusions into workers' trade union rights, a precedent that would have been without *any* justification had the NDP only been prepared to go as far as the P.Q.'s anti-scab legislation. The Manitoba reform experience in the mid-1980s, in this respect, provides a disturbing example of the impact of the new coercive measures in redrawing the limits of reform.

These limits are also visible when we turn to the record of Ontario's minority Liberal government, elected in May 1985. On the positive side, in addition to pay equity legislation (Bill 154) and severance pay and pension reforms, the Peterson Government also passed Bill 65, amending the *Labour Relations Act* to provide for the imposition of first agreements by the Labour Relations Board. Moreover, the actual terms and conditions under which first agreements are to be imposed met strong approval from organized labour.[61] However, given the limits of first agreement legislation noted above, other developments which have not involved new legislation are more important. Recent rulings by the Ontario Labour Relations Board have supported union demands for broader based bargaining as a means of redressing weakness due to fragmented bargaining-unit structures; and have extended striking workers' right to return to their jobs beyond the old six month limit.[62] Equally significant, perhaps, were the changes within the Department of Labour where a number of senior bureaucrats, including long-time deputy minister Tim Armstrong, have effectively been forced out.[63] A former law partner of David Lewis and leading legal adviser for the UAW, Armstrong had developed a good working relationship with provincial labour leaders. The latter obtained a voice in departmental affairs, including appointments to various public bodies, in exchange for muted opposition to government policy, particularly in the area of workplace health and safety but also with respect to the denial of the right to strike to public sector workers. In other words, the industrial unions' considerable political influence *within* the Ontario Department of Labour was purchased at the cost of ignoring (and at times suppressing) rank-and-file challenges to managerial prerogatives. Nor did they, despite all the rhetoric about solidarity, influence an attempt to overcome Premier Davis's implacable refusal to even countenance discussions about Ontario civil servants or hospital workers obtaining the right to strike, even after OPSEU and the hospital unions made this a priority. The defeat of the Davis government called this relationship into question. Peterson's appointment of the progressive and able Bill Wrye as Minister of Labour meant that some reform was inevitable. A clean-up in the area of health and safety, given the growing pressure from the rank-and-file and the press (thanks especially to the initiative of OPSEU whose members include health and safety inspectors), was clearly on the political agenda. So was first contract legislation—both of which Armstrong had strongly opposed. Ultimately, it became a matter of either Wrye or Armstrong leaving; it was certainly significant that it was Armstrong who went.

Nevertheless, the fact remains that the list of items on the reform agenda has not been terribly long. Conspicuous in its absence, at least to date, is the most outstanding issue of all—the blanket denial of the right to strike, under any circumstances, for provincial government employees and hospital workers. Like other provincial governments, even with explicitly different ideological predispositions, the Liberals were apparently unmoved by the ILO's ruling that this proscription violated its Convention 87 on freedom of association, to which Canada is a signatory. At the same time, it needs to be noted that even under the Liberal-NDP accord, coercion remained present alongside reform. As if not to be outdone by the preceding Conservative government—which in its last days passed two pieces of back-to-work legislation (one of which, in honour of the Pope's visit, pre-emptively denied Toronto Transit Commission workers the right to strike)—the Liberals, in their first year in office, also passed such legislation on two occasions.

The Peterson Government's own use of back-to-work legislation, not surprisingly, signalled to some that little would change under the Liberals. Its common use throughout Canada over the past decade has to be seen, not only in terms of workers whose strike rights it directly suspends, but also of its indirect effects of intimidating other workers who fear its application as well. It made many managers in the public sector much less prepared to engage in serious bargaining in the expectation that a long public sector strike would elicit a back-to-work measure from governments. This was graphically visible in Ontario during the Metro Toronto teachers' strike in the fall of 1987, over the issue of more preparation time for lessons. Despite considerable public sympathy for the teachers, the Board of Education took a hard line. Board Chairwoman, Anne Vanstone, told reporters that she was prepared to wait for back-to-work legislation from the government while a number of her counterparts took the opportunity to call for "a better mechanism for settling disputes" than the strike.[64] Significantly, the Peterson Government, by this time having been returned to office with a large majority, did not rise to the bait on this occasion. The teachers were able to secure a settlement that went some way to meeting their demands. Whether this foretells a clear break with past practices; and above all, whether it proves to be a signal that the pressure again being applied by a coalition of unions, demanding the right to strike for hospital workers and civil servants in Ontario, will finally bear fruit under the Liberals, will be important to watch for.

Whatever the outcome, it is also significant that the core private sector industrial unions in Ontario have been spared the kind of restrictive state legislation visited on others through the 1980s. Apart from the differing ideological dispositions of a Peterson-style as opposed to a Vander Zalm-style provincial government, the main reason for this relates to the specific material conditions of the Ontario economy, with manufacturing industry and financial capital centred there. The importance of manufacturing in Ontario means that the over-all tone of government policies, *vis-à-vis* labour, is determined more by considerations pertaining to the industrial unions than in other provinces, where public sector or resource unions are core to the labour movement. Restrictive legislation against public employees in Ontario does not itself provide the signal to capital that the government "means business;" yet, subjecting the core industrial unions in Ontario to restrictive legislation is more fraught with problems than taking on public employees.

In any case, the Ontario government has had more room to manoeuvre by virtue of the manufacturing industry's recovery after 1982 (aided by the labour cost advantage which a low exchange rate relative to the American dollar has yielded) as well as by Toronto, specifically, benefitting from financial capital's speculative romp through the 1980s. At the same time, the leading role industrial unions themselves played in collective bargaining in the earlier era has been much constrained in a new era of capitalist restructuring and the heightened competition that produced it. Operating under the old legal framework, and in the context of Ontario's relatively robust economy, real wages, even amongst the autoworkers (that weathervane of the Canadian labour movement), have hardly gone up through the 1980s. So, even if such unions are militant, as the autoworkers have been, they seem unable to do much more than keep pace with inflation. We shall take up the consequences of this more broadly in the concluding chapter. Suffice to say here that this does *not* mean that these unions have been rendered ineffectual. In so far as workers have maintained living standards, this itself indicates that there is still power in the union. Moreover, in the context of international capitalist competition, the existence of solid shop-floor organization poses a barrier to attempts at restructuring.

We have seen the federal government move to break this power in the Crown corporations, and this has obviously affected a great many workers who live in Ontario. But there are limits to doing this in the private sector, at least in the industrial heartland of Ontario and, arguably, to a lesser extent in Quebec. Notwithstanding the sections of capital lobbying for this to be applied to the private sector, and given the substantial profits underwritten by Canada's low exchange rate, their claims that government inaction against industrial unions leads to massive capital outflow do not persuade the public or governments lacking in neo-conservative fervor. These governments are concerned by the political repercussions of struggles that labour undertook elsewhere and that would certainly be undertaken by the industrial unions in Ontario, were there a direct state assault on their right to strike.

It is for this reason, in large measure, that manufacturing capital supports free trade. It obviously suits capitalists who profit directly from Canada's resource exports, and fits with financial capital's world-wide drive to break down the autonomy of national government economic policy. Free trade endangers manufacturing industries in Canada by rendering them more open to competition. Yet, capital hopes to achieve, through enhanced flexibility regarding plant locations and sourcing of inputs that free trade will bring, the breaking of union power that has occurred in the United States. Continued worker resistance, in the context of the free trade accord, would make capital's pressure on the state to fill the crucial gaps remaining in the post-controls period much more effective. Should this happen, the brunt of our analysis clearly indicates that there is now a strong juridical basis for the widespread extension of limitations on the right to strike, from the public to the private sector. It is not only the immediate protection of jobs, but the protection of their basic democratic freedoms, that hangs in the balance for Ontario's industrial workers in the context of free trade.

Pay Equity

What remains to be considered is the pay equity legislation of the 1980s, which most observers would treat as the most significant legislative reform of the decade. Pay equity legislation does not expand union rights, but it is an important response to the long-standing efforts of the women's movement, outside and in the labour movement, to reduce the large disparity between male and female earnings. Pay equity measures address the contribution to this inequality due to discrimination—the adverse impact on women's earnings due to the systemic devaluation of women's work—by seeking to ensure that jobs of comparable value carry equal rates of pay. In essence, the legislation: specifies the basis for determining the value of a job (typically as a composite of skill, effort, responsibility and working conditions); requires the establishment of a system for evaluating jobs; and, sets out a procedure for eliminating existing differences in pay for jobs of equal value by raising the rate of the lower-paid job. Beyond this, the different Acts set out the terms and conditions governing the application of these basic principles, varying substantially in their restrictiveness. Our discussion of the significance of these restrictions, and of pay equity legislation generally, will focus on the two most far-reaching Acts, those in Manitoba and Ontario.[65]

While these Acts are "proactive" in the sense of requiring employers within their purview to establish pay equity plans, the Manitoba legislation is unique in providing for a Pay Equity Bureau empowered to initiate complaints. However, the Act, like those in P.E.I. and New Brunswick, applies only to the public sector, offering no benefit at all to the most poorly-paid segments of the female workforce. Ontario's act is much broader, extending to large parts of the private sector, but it still ignores the most impoverished women by excluding companies with fewer than ten employees and is only voluntary for those with less than a hundred employees. Moreover, the Pay Equity Commission's role is defined as passive. While employers are required to develop and post plans for achieving pay equity, any plan is automatically deemed to be approved unless the employees file a complaint; only then does the Commission get involved. In all these Acts, comparisons between male and female pay rates are confined to a single establishment, thereby having little impact on women in workplaces which are virtually entirely female (e.g. daycares, nursing homes, libraries and clothing factories). Furthermore, both Acts, generally, allow only for comparisons between "female-dominated" and "male-dominated" jobs (i.e. where 60-70 per cent of employees are of the same sex)—although Manitoba's Act specifically allows for other comparisons—further narrowing the scope and benefits of the legislation.

Despite its broader scope, the Ontario legislation has a particularly narrow view of pay equity, requiring only that the top rates of female- and male-dominated jobs be equal. Inequities due to merit pay, skill shortages, seniority and temporary training assignments are expressly permitted. Finally, both Acts put a cap on the cost of pay equity to employers, limiting annual adjustments to 1 per cent of payroll costs. Ontario defines these costs as exclusive of benefits, with no limit on the number of adjustments which may be necessary to achieve pay equity; Manitoba provides no definition of payroll costs, but allows for only four years of adjustment.

The web of restrictions reviewed above show pay equity legislation to be a limited instrument for reform. However, a further crucial limitation remains to be considered: for all practical purposes, these pay equity measures mainly pertain to organized women workers. This is the case for Manitoba, notwithstanding the proactive nature of its legislation, by virtue of its scope being limited to the highly-organized public sector. In Ontario, it arises from the passive posture of the Commission charged with enforcing the Act, given the traditional (and understandable) reluctance of unorganized workers to file complaints against their employers, since these workers don't have a union to protect them.[66] A growing body of research, mainly by feminists, suggests that a significant portion of the wage gap may be due to women's relative lack of bargaining power. For example, recent studies show that the pay of organized women far exceeds that of their unorganized sisters. Mary Cornish has pointed out that "on average a woman's pay goes up by $3.35 per hour or 43 per cent if her job is unionized. No other single step is likely to bring about a greater increase in pay."[67] Since this difference among women workers is larger than that between organized and unorganized workers overall, it suggests that the wage gap is most likely to be narrowed primarily through organizing, rather than pay equity legislation.

In any case, the significance of the legislation for women will certainly depend very much on the political process within unions. In this respect, note that, if the legislation has the beneficial effect of promoting pay equity in the unions, it may also have the untoward effect of constraining the responses of unions to it. The Manitoba and Ontario Acts require that unions agree to the job evaluation scheme adopted, with provision for binding arbitration in the event agreement proves impossible. Job evaluation, however, is an exceedingly subjective process. The measures selected to determine the various value criteria set out in the Acts, the weight given them in constructing the index and the jobs selected for comparison will determine how much "pay discrimination" exists. If the position of the employer on how to proceed is obvious, that of the union is not. Particularly (but not only) in the private sector, where the corporate bottom line sets a limit on wage increases, gains for some female workers may well be at the expense of other (male and/or female) workers, ensuring that the process of arriving at a position will hardly be smooth.

Over the past decade, feminists have made the needs of women workers much more salient in a number of unions. In the process, they have developed new strategies for advancing these needs, partly to overcome the divisions which demands such as equal pay for work of equal value exposed in the unions. In CUPE, for example, feminists led in the development of a bargaining strategy which gave priority to the upward reclassification of low-paid jobs and flat-rate rather than percentage pay increases. By making the problem one of low pay, a concern of many men as well as women, they found a more effective strategy for advancing the interests of women.

When placed in this context, pay equity legislation, paradoxically, may even have perverse effects. On the one hand, it can short-circuit the political process underway in the unions, by creating an excuse for taking the issue out of the union/collective bargaining process (including demand formulation) and putting it into the lap of outside job evaluation "experts." There is evidence that this is already happening. As one CUPE representative has told us, "We're devoting all our efforts to the legislation. It has made the issue so complex and confusing. Most of the time in educational work is spent explaining the legislation. CUPE's collective bargaining strategy has taken second place."[68] On the other hand, an employer faced with a union determined to narrow the range of job classifications (recall CUPW's successful fight in the 1970s against Canada Post's attempt to introduce a new lower job classification for work on automated sorting machines) could use the legislation—with its provision for binding arbitration where no appropriate job evaluation agreement can be reached—to block any real advance. Whether this will actually occur remains to be seen, but the possibility cannot be ignored as an aspect of the limits of reform in the late 1980s and beyond.

In saying this we don't deny that such reforms, however limited, *can* be beneficial. Still, this will largely depend on the unions' capacity to *make* them so. This, in turn, will depend on the capacity of unions to resist attacks on their collective power and to develop effective counter-strategies. It is the issues raised by these questions that we will explore in the concluding chapter.

CHAPTER 6

The Labour Movement in the New Era: Back to the Future

Right now we are in a situation where there is a need for a national debate on the issue... [but] the weakness is really that the leadership is not going to the membership to lead. Too many leaders say the membership is not ready ... but I think the leadership has to come out: they are not leading.... [I]t starts with a feeling of being powerless. So why do they feel powerless? Well first of all, the big thing is that we are fighting the government and fighting against the law. So you get the feeling, how can I do something? If you meet with lawyers two or three times in a week, they are not going to tell you that you have to fight in the streets. They are going to tell you what the legal avenues are, and so you get directed to that. And then, in addition, many leaders have no control over the unions. When I say control, I mean that it's not even controlled by the members either. The structure is made in such a way that in order for the leaders to get to the membership, they have to go through a structure, and never get to the membership, which is a serious problem. Especially at a time when you have to work with other unions ... the structure of the labour movement is unbelievable. People don't seem to know what to do. It's like the leadership has never gotten involved in a struggle before. It seems you have to go through all the ABC's of what a struggle is in order to get organized. Amazing! Probably a lack of willingness is some part of this, not only a feeling of being powerless. Of course, there is also a question of policies. Some unions don't develop policies. They don't know where to go because they haven't adopted a direction to take. You also have a situation where the policies are developed at the CLC or the provincial federations of labour—some are followed, some are not—but these are seen as CLC or OFL policies; they are not the union's policies. This is another reason why the leadership feels powerless.

C. Parrot [1]

How has the labour movement responded to the new era? "Free collective bargaining" was rooted in a material basis of consent given by the expansion of post-war capitalism. As this stage drew to a close in the 1970s, the material basis of consent became more fragile. If this prepared the ground for the turn to coercion, it also opened space for resistance to such coercion, resistance determined by organizational, political and ideological factors as well as economic ones. It is this resistance, actual and potential, that we finally need to explore.

One must never fall into the unidimensional and ultimately defeatist perspective of ascribing monolithic power to, or even overestimating the dominance of, capital and the state. The relations of class power in a capitalist society are asymmetric; nevertheless, the power that inheres in collective labour always remains a constituent element of such a society, and it is upon this basis that the potential for social change arises. The legal framework of collective bargaining established in the 1940s—so well-described by Rand as "machinery devised to adjust toward increasing harmony" the interests of labour, capital and the state—still left capital occupying the "dominant position." This had been supplemented in the 1960s by further reforms such as the famous Woods Task Force on Labour Relations in 1968, which had frankly described them as the "means of legitimizing and making more acceptable the superior-subordinate nexus inherent in the employer-employee relationship." Despite these reforms, it still proved no easy task to "domesticate" and "housebreak" the unions and fit "them into the national family as one of the tame cats."

As we have seen, class struggle had continued, and even increased, through the course of the era of free collective bargaining. Indeed, it could be argued that the fact of ongoing class struggle in a changed economic climate largely prompted attempts to increase capital's hegemony through legalistic coercion. To be sure, this limited and sectionalized struggle was underwritten and institutionalized by the legal and institutional matrix of collective bargaining. This framework certainly limited the mobilizing capacity of unions. It even played a not inconsiderable role in marginalizing the kind of socialist vision and purpose that had helped fuel the labour movement's organizational struggles of the 1930s and 1940s. The Canadian labour movement in the following decades mainly undertook such struggles as could be advanced within the parameters of "actually-existing capitalism." This left unchallenged the underlying structural asymmetry of power between capital and labour inherent in capitalism. Thus, the ground always remained in place for capital and the state to effect the assault on free collective bargaining that emerged in the new economic, political and ideological conditions of the 1970s and 1980s.

This did not mean that the conditions for class struggle were closed off in and against the new era of coercion, not least because it contained its own contradictions. If the new economic conditions made workers less secure in their jobs and undermined their confidence in wage militancy, it also meant that union organization and rights became more important for workers to protect their jobs and material conditions. Moreover, such economic contradictions were overlaid with ideological ones. Capitalism's claim on workers' consent in the Cold War had been sustained, in part, not only by the rising standards of living in the West, but also by the post-war settlement's legal proclamation of workers' democratic rights—while pointing to the travesty of democratic rights in authoritarian Communist regimes. Fighting the new Cold War at the onset of the 1980s, Western governments praised the struggle of the Solidarity movement in Poland to secure freedom of association for Polish workers; *at the same time*, these governments were circumscribing or denying the rights of workers in their own countries. Canadian workers could be excused if they misread editorials on "the rebirth of the trade union movement" in Poland as speaking to their own circumstances. Ideological conditions were not entirely propitious for convincingly selling the new coercion to Canadian workers in the name of voluntarism and freedom. Considerable ideological space existed for unions to mobilize workers' struggles against the new coercion.

It is usually assumed that in introducing strike restrictions, Canadian governments are responding to public opinion. It suits governments, and their apologists in the media, to foster this impression; but, is this true in fact? It would be folly to deny public impatience with strikes—sometimes raised to a fever pitch by business, government and media bias against public sector strikes. Yet, Gallup polls over the last decade show "there has been a steady increase in the level of support nationally for the right of workers to strike."[2] A poll conducted in March 1987, found 68 per cent of Canadians thought workers should have the right to strike, compared with 56 per cent in 1981 (note that had the right to strike been included in the Charter, it would have reflected majority opinion even then). This is not to say that most people consider the right to strike absolute. With the emotive phrase "essential services" added to the question, in 1987 only 36 per cent felt workers performing those services should have that right. This is still up sharply from 23 per cent in 1981, suggesting that more Canadians realize that governments use "essential services" as an excuse, and undertake unjustified incursions on the right to strike. This trend is likely to grow since *the support for the right to strike is twice as strong among people under fifty than those over fifty years of age*. Also, no less than 83 per cent of people living in union households believe workers should have the right to strike and 52 per cent of them say they should have it even in "essential services."

It should be clear from our account of the evolution of the new era of coercion that the labour movement has not simply lain down and played dead. Even as the economic crisis deepened, Canadian unions were less cowed, by their employers *and* the state, than their American counterparts. This was seen, above all, as the autoworkers in Canada (whose key industrial location and organizational and ideological influence always makes them a weathervane for developments in the labour movement) developed a strategy, from the late 1970s onwards, for non-concession bargaining. This set them on a very different course from the American wing of the international union. It symbolized a much broader set of impressions, on both sides of the border, about the more militant nature of the Canadian labour movement. Remarkably, while the American media in the early

1980s focussed on Chrysler's Lee Iaccoca as the most charismatic figure in industry, the Canadian media attributed a similar aura of charisma, not to a *capitalist* , but to a *union leader* , the UAW 's Bob White. Canadian public employees at the turn of the decade also appeared less frightened by threats of public sector cutbacks than were such workers in the United States, evidenced in a number of public sector strikes, most notably by nurses in Alberta, hospital workers in Ontario, and federal clerical workers. (Although it should be noted that even in the 1979-81 period, when the public sector was free of wage controls, it still did not lead the private sector in wage increases.[3])

The number of union members in the United States has declined continually since the mid-1950s: membership accounted for 35 per cent of the non-agricultural labour force in the mid-1950s, 29 per cent in the mid-1960s, 25 per cent in the mid-1970s, and fell to below 18 per cent by 1986. Canadian union membership trends diverged sharply from the 1960s onwards. Although membership fell from 34 per cent in 1954 to just under 30 per cent by 1963, it grew from that point on and reached 39 per cent by 1978. It fell slightly over the following three years, but then rebounded to 40 per cent by 1983. (See Table VII.)

The contrast between the U.S. and Canadian experience since the 1960s is often drawn in terms of public sector unionism having "made a greater quantitative difference in Canada than the U.S. [but] it also appears to have made a greater qualitative difference, strengthening the elements of aggressiveness and competitiveness in the movement. The Canadian labor mobilization of the mid-1960s, which changed the condition of private sector unionism as well, is unthinkable without the activities of employees in the public sector".[4] This

TABLE VII
Union Membership In Canada and the United States 1955-86

Year	Total Membership (,000)		As a % of Non-Agricultural Workers	
	Canada	U.S.	Canada	U.S.
1955	1,268	16,127	33.7	31.8
1960	1,459	15,516	32.3	28.6
1965	1,589	18,269	29.7	30.1
1970	2,173	20,990	33.6	29.6
1975	2,884	22,207	36.9	28.9
1978	3,278	21,757	39.0	25.1
1981	3,487	20,647	37.4	22.6
1982	3,617	19,571	39.0	21.9
1983	3,563	17,717	40.0	20.4
1984	3,651	17,340	39.6	19.1
1985	3,666	16,996	39.0	18.3
1986	3,730	16,975	37.7	17.8

Source: The Current Industrial Relations Scene in Canada, 1987 Queen's Industrial Relations Centre, Reference Tables, p. 362.

development started a rapid decline of the proportion of Canadian union members belonging to international (read American) unions. Whereas 70 per cent belonged to the latter from 1950 to 1965, only 50 per cent did a decade later, and by the mid-1980s this figure fell to less than 40 per cent. Especially in the 1980s, this dramatic change pertained less to the relative growth of organized public sector workers in Canada, but to disaffiliation of Canadian sections from the Internationals. Although this reflected growing political differences, including a distinctive nationalist turn in ideological dispositions, it grew directly out of divergent collective bargaining strategies between the Canadian sections and the American headquarters. This was itself reflective of the greater militancy and capacity for struggle in the Canadian labour movement.

It is well beyond the scope of this study to attempt to account for the difference between Canadian and American unions in this period; above all, the reasons are inseparable from the historical development of the working classes, as well as of the state and the labour relations regime in each country.[5] While the difference between union orientation in the two countries is real enough, it should not lead to Panglossian celebrations regarding the strength or well-being of labour in Canada. This only seems to be the case if we take the sorry experience of American labour as a benchmark: *in contrast with an American union movement on its knees, our's is bound to look tall.* Such celebrations of the Canadian labour movement's well-being either ignore or make light of the turn to coercion and the devaluing of union rights described in this book. The most that can be said is that while Canadian capitalists still strongly and effectively resisted unionization in the service sector (to which the first-contract legislation of a number of Canadian jurisdictions has been, as we have seen, a quite inadequate response), they have not been able as yet—at least outside of construction—to go very far in ridding themselves of unions.

Union density in Canada *has* fallen slightly since 1983. The kind of legislation introduced in British Columbia in 1987 (where union density fell from 46 per cent in 1982 to just under 40 per cent today—the lowest for forty years) can only make matters worse. So will the current restructuring of public enterprises and, perhaps even more so, the installation of free trade. But the important point is this: the continuing contrast with U.S. labour *does* speak to the greater potential for collective struggle by Canadian workers. Just this, also speaks to the need felt by many elements among capital and the state in Canada to police union freedoms more effectively, keeping pace in this way with what has taken place in the imperial heartland. This especially applies to the public sector unions who have borne the brunt of new labour legislation. It helps explain why through the 1980s the Canadian state moved to restrict significantly, not the *number* of union members in the public sector, but rather the *rights* that makes such union membership effective.

Seen in this light, the Canadian labour movement has had little to celebrate in terms of conventional collective bargaining objectives. After the nominally high wage increases secured in the early 1970s (increases in weekly earnings averaged 10.2 per cent from 1971 to 1975), the length and breadth of the wage deceleration since 1975 has been unprecedented. The growth in average weekly earnings fell: first, to 8.7 per cent from 1975 to 1981; continued to fall through the "6 and 5" controls period and fell further still in the mid-1980s (in 1984, the rate of increase in average weekly earnings stood at 4.3 per cent, falling to 3.5 per cent in 1985 and 2.8 per cent in 1986). Adjusting for inflation, real wages actually entered a sustained period of decline after 1975; which continued into the 1980s, even as the rate of inflation itself began to decline. This has continued, despite the fact that unemployment finally began to decline in the mid-1980s (real weekly earnings declined on average by -0.1 per cent in 1984, by -0.5 per cent in 1985, and by -1.3 per cent in 1986). Even in Ontario, where unemployment has almost fallen to average post-war levels, the rate of wage increases still did not exceed 4 per cent in 1986. Most workers were failing to keep pace with a rate of inflation of 4.2 per cent. In B.C. and Alberta, with a much worse unemployment situation, money wage increases were less than 1 per cent in 1986 (some two-thirds of private sector agreements in Western Canada installed wage freezes or cuts). Workers' real incomes fell drastically, even leaving aside the income and sales tax increases that have impinged heavily on unionized workers in recent years. Since 1983, union wage increases in Canada have actually lagged behind non-union increases and the wage gap between unionized and non-unionized workers decreased. As one close observer pointed out, "It is a myth that Canadian unions, unlike their counterparts have not made concessions. They have not made as many or as deep concessions, but they have had to make some."[6]

The consolidation of permanent exceptionalism in the 1980s has coincided with a decline in strike activity as well as real wages (see Table VIII). Through the late 1970s and into the first two years of the 1980s, the number of strikes and of workers involved fell back somewhat—from a peak of about twelve hundred strikes with over a half-million workers involved in both 1974 and 1975, to about a thousand strikes with some four hundred thousand workers involved in both 1980 and 1981. Since then, economic conditions as well as legal restrictions on strike activity have had real effects. The number of strikes ranged between six hundred and fifty and eight hundred and twenty-five per year from 1982 to 1985, with a sharply decreasing number of workers involved (from over four hundred thousand in 1982 to approximately a hundred and fifty thousand in 1985).

Still, it is clear that there has been no return to the quiescent industrial relations of the 1950s. The defense of existing standards and the increasing necessity for unions to strike for first contracts for newly-organized groups, has meant that strike activity in the 1980s stood well above even the rapidly rising levels of the early to mid-1960s. In 1986, there were strong indications of even more determined militancy, albeit mostly defensive, designed to prevent massive cut-backs as in the tenacious struggle of the Gainer's workers in Alberta against Peter Pocklington, or to undo coercive legislation as in the illegal nape strike in Newfoundland. Workers' will to struggle has not been quashed in Canada, that much is clear. No less clear, the Canadian labour movement at all levels has proved incapable (since the turn to permanent exceptionalism in the mid-1970s and right through its consolidation in the 1980s) of sustained, coordinated defense—industrially, politically, or ideologically—against the political encroachments on fundamental union freedoms that we have outlined in this book.

It is remarkable how unprepared the Canadian labour movement has been for each successive blow struck by the state. Nor has it proved capable of mounting

TABLE VIII
Strikes and Lockouts in Canada 1975-85

Year	Number	Workers Involved	Persondays	% Estimated Working Time
1975	1,171	506,443	10,908,810	0.53
1976	1,039	1,570,940	11,609,890	0.55
1977	803	217,557	3,307,880	0.15
1978	1,058	401,688	7,392,820	0.34
1979	1,050	462,504	7,834,230	0.34
1980	1,028	441,025	8,975,390	0.38
1981	1,048	338,548	8,878,490	0.37
1982	677	444,302	5,795,420	0.25
1983	645	329,309	4,443,960	0.19
1984	717	186,755	3,871,820	0.16
1985	825	159,727	3,180,710	0.13

Source: Labour Canada, *Strikes and Lockouts in Canada* (1985), p. 9.

any meaningful or sustained counter-offensive. To be sure, the national one-day general strike organized by the Canadian Labour Congress against the Anti-Inflation Programme, the "Day of Protest" of October 14, 1976, was an early indication of the labour movement's unwillingness to succumb to the first salvos of the new era of coercion. Yet, the 1976 Day of Protest—while in itself a successful and unprecedented mobilization—was, after all, the climax of real opposition by the CLC to the Anti-Inflation Programme, rather than the onset of a campaign of sustained and effective struggle against it. The CLC appeared confused, ideologically and strategically: it wavered between advancing illusionary corporatist schemes for tripartite business, labour and government planning of the economy, on the one hand; and, on the other hand, in the course of the CLC's unsuccessful constitutional challenge of the Programme, it brought a leading liberal economist, Richard Lipsey, before the Supreme Court to make a free market case against wage and price controls.

As the 1970s drew to a close, the CLC leadership's continuing illusions regarding the state's commitment to the old legal framework (even when back-to-work legislation abrogated the workers' rights contained therein), was strikingly illustrated by its abandonment of—indeed Dennis McDermott's explicit attack on—the postal workers, in 1978. In fact, Jean Claude Parrot went to jail in 1979 for having refused to counsel his members to go back to work, as the state required of him, in the face of specific legislation which removed from postal workers the rights guaranteed them by general legislation. There was little evidence that the labour movement as a whole had much understanding or any great concern regarding the issues at stake, or what it suggested about broader developments in train. It is true that in advance of the federal government's "6 and 5" legislation, a resolution calling for action—up to and including a general strike—in the event that the government abrogated the right to strike, was carried by a huge majority at the CLC convention. Yet, the sound and fury signified little in the end. The CLC leadership was not wrong in recognizing that such resolutions—full of rhetorical flourish—failed to address the means to ensure that such a call would secure mass support. When "6 and 5" did materialize, the CLC hesitantly established a committee to coordinate the response of public sector unions.[7] However, none of the major unions was able, even where willing, to mobilize their members in that summer and fall of 1982.

Particularly surprising, despite the repeated attacks on the right to strike in the late 1970s, the CLC was virtually alone among large interest groups in Canada, in remaining aloof from the constitutional debate at the beginning of the 1980s. It was, in any case, indicative of the labour movement's trenchant economism, its subordinate consciousness to the exclusion of a hegemonic orientation, that it regarded the debate over the constitution and the Charter as nothing more than an ideological smokescreen. It did not even intervene in the debate attempting to clarify why they thought this was so—at an apt moment in Canadian history to raise profound issues regarding the limited and cramped nature of Canadian democracy. Even in terms of the immediate interests of the unions, one might have expected, at least, they would make representations to the parliamentary hearings regarding inclusion of the right to strike (or free collective bargaining or full employment) in the Charter. A few other liberal democratic constitutions (such as Italy and France, reflecting the influence of Communist parties in those countries at the time these constitutions were drafted) refer to such rights. Although the practical effect of constitutional phrases may not, of themselves, be great, inclusion of such rights at least furthers their legitimacy within the framework of political discourse, and thus, may help unions in gaining support when it comes to struggles defending or extending such rights. It was unlikely that a campaign to include such rights in the Charter would be successful. At the very least, it would have put the issue on the political agenda and perhaps made Canadians more sensitive to the attack on these rights in the 1980s.

For various reasons, quite apart from any sensitivity to the limits of legalization of politics and trade unionism, the CLC did not act. Undoubtedly, the reasons for this inaction included: a traditional economism; the federal NDP 's alliance with the Liberals, on the Constitution; as well as the Quebec Federation of Labour's reluctance to improve a Constitution which the government fundamentally opposed. Yet, the same day the Justice Minister announced Charter amendments in response to submissions by over a hundred groups across the country (but no unions), the National Union of Provincial Government Employees announced that it would seek action from the Labour Minister, in the wake of the ILO ruling sustaining a CLC complaint regarding Alberta's violations of freedom of association for its public employees. Would the CLC have been less myopic and complacent about the Constitutional debate, knowing that, two months after its proclamation, the right to strike would be "temporarily" removed from federal employees, and indeed, shortly thereafter from most provincial employees, as well?

Among those sympathetic to labour's rights, some are suspicious of the legalization of politics which an entrenched bill of rights can entail, and of the expansion of judiciary powers in relation to its review of parliamentary legislation.[8] They are concerned that unions will allow their over-all strategies to be defined by lawyers; and that support for the institutionalization of judicial review will leave a socialist government without recourse when the judiciary, as is likely, defends the rights of property against a radical government. Unfortunately, such concerns are sometimes mixed up with a picture drawn of parliamentary democracy which obscures the centralization of state power in the executive and bureaucracy, and which fails to envision the broadening of democracy beyond the act of voting for hierarchically structured parties every four or five years. Moreover, this position tends to foreclose the question of whether freedom of association, with all it entails, needs to be constitutionally guaranteed, even in a socialist society.

Ultimately, the effective defence of union freedoms does not lie in representation to parliamentary committees on constitutional rights or in appeals to the courts. Yet, it would be utterly unrealistic to expect the union movement to abstain entirely from defending their rights in the juridical arena after the Charter was passed. The point of a CLC campaign specifying that freedom of association should explicitly include the right to strike would have been to some extent— partly through the Charter but even more through the campaign itself—to limit the judiciary as much as the legislative and executive apparatus of the state. At the very least, the unions could have tried to ensure that legislative attacks on the right to strike could be constitutionally permissible only if they could be shown to fall within the exceptional limits on fundamental freedoms, provided under Section 1 of the Charter. As it was, it was left open to the judiciary to find— predictably enough, given the lack of specification and the judiciary's orientation—that freedom of association did not guarantee the right to strike at all, and thus further facilitate, juridically and ideologically, the consolidation of permanent exceptionalism.

Had the CLC seen that the Charter would enmesh class struggles even further in the legal process, there might have been some defensible rationale for its position. But no such case was made or, apparently, even contemplated. On the contrary, the CLC, like most of its member unions, accepted the legal framework they had become enmeshed in and turned to the courts in an entirely tactical fashion—ignoring the strategic reorientation the constitutional debate momentarily provided. The CLC *had* challenged the Anti-Inflation controls of 1975 before the Supreme Court, on much less lofty principles than freedom of association (the powers of the provinces in the labour field had to be the main grounds for a constitutional challenge at that time). Even before the ink on the Charter was barely dry, they were using its vague freedom of association provision in court appeals against continuing government transgressions of the right to strike. It was also inevitable that capital would use the Charter to secure judicial rulings against labour, in terms of the liberal individualist philosophy that the Charter espouses; and it was just as inevitable that the unions would attempt to defend themselves against this. The real issue is *how* they go about this: whether they allow lawyers to determine their over-all strategy; whether they confuse the individualistic and defensive arguments they are forced to make in the courts with the message they deliver to their members; and whether they spend an inordinate amount of their energies and resources in this arena. To the extent they do this, they reduce their capacity to apply the most effective union response to state and employer attacks—the mobilization and political education of their own membership.

The labour movement's failure to mobilize effective opposition against each component of the new era of coercion has, perhaps, best been accounted for by J.C. Parrot in the quotation that opens this chapter. The leadership's lack of will to fight the legislative onslaught against the right to strike relentlessly, is itself the product of a deeper problem. As Parrot pointed out, a "sense of powerlessness" showed itself through the inability to mobilize the membership toward the co-ordinated, political and solidaristic—rather than sectional and economistic—struggles required by conditions in the 1980s. Their sense of powerlessness was, of course, proportional to the magnitude of the task they now faced. However, the most powerful section of the labour movement, the auto and steel unions in Ontario, did not go out of their way to ensure that public sector workers would obtain the right to strike in that province, even in the 1960s and early 1970s. Was it likely that they would rise up to defend the attacks on the right to strike in the late 1970s and 1980s? Was it likely that a weak and ideologically confused central labour federation like the CLC would suddenly find the capacity, not just to mediate such sectionalism, but to overcome it and lead a co-ordinated struggle? Such sectionalism was itself the result of years of neglect of the political and ideological mobilizing aspects of trade unionism—leading to years of legalistic practice. This had taken its toll on the capacity of the labour movement to undertake an effectively solidaristic political struggle. As Parrot put it, "You meet with lawyers, you meet with government representatives, and if you don't go back to the source, the membership, you are going to become a technical, legal guy. You can forget about the real struggle...."[9] So, even where the necessity of "going back to the source" and reinvigorating the struggle was recognized by growing elements among the leadership, the structures and habits of the labour movement were ill-suited to it. First, the leadership and the membership had to find a way to relearn the "ABC's of what a struggle is," especially what a political struggle is.

It was only in British Columbia, with the emergence of the Solidarity Coalition against the provincial government's package of reactionary measures in July 1983, that the possibility emerged of making credible the threat of a general strike, raised at the CLC convention earlier in the year. The initial orientation in B.C. in the summer and fall of 1983 transcended the traditional institutional and ideological divisions within the labour movement, and between it and radical social activists—a remarkable development. Solidarity's campaign of mass demonstrations and a planned escalation of political strikes compelled the British Columbia government to retreat (abandoning Bill 2 and agreeing to wholesale exemptions from Bill 3, two of the most repressive elements of its July package). Nonetheless, the deal struck between the B.C. Federation of Labour and the Bennett Government exemplified the fundamental problems we have mentioned. The deal not only set aside the broader welfare and human rights issues which were an integral part of the struggle, but also left unresolved the demands of the workers who led the strike in the education sector. The deal was made behind the backs of the other groups associated with the Coalition and without consulting the union membership, either. As we have seen, it did not slow down the wave of coercive legislation that continued to rain on B.C. unions.

Had the B.C. Federation allowed the escalating strikes to continue, they could possibly have secured a greater retreat from the July measures and forewarned the Socreds and other Canadian governments, against further packages of this kind.[10] Clearly, most of the leadership—given that they didn't want a general strike, fearing it would lead to charges of "anarchy" and harm the electoral prospects of the NDP—found it useful to underestimate the militancy of the membership and to overestimate the tenacity of the government even in the face of evidence to the contrary. A political perspective marked by overarching electoralism led to the extra-parliamentary mobilization of the Coalition being set aside in favour of relying on the electoral prospects of the NDP "next time." There were strong feelings of betrayal, not only among the radical social activists, but also in the B.C. Federation of Labour itself; as was seen when the most visible agent of the compromise, Jack Munro of the Woodworkers, suffered a stunning defeat in the executive elections at the 1984 Federation convention.

After Bill Vander Zalm emerged, dashing the NDP chances in the 1986 provincial election, and after his electoral promises of industrial conciliation took shape in the form of the repressive Bills 19 and 20; all the questions set aside in 1983 had to be faced again. A young new leadership, schooled in the student and labour activism of the 1960s, now led the Federation. Even though they had made their peace with the Woodworkers and brought Munro back into the Federation executive, they appeared more in tune with the spirit that had infused the Solidarity Coalition. The B.C. Federation of Labour organized a series of regional protests and a very successful one-day general strike on June 1, 1987, when no less than three hundred thousand workers brought the province to a halt, and by all accounts enjoyed remarkable public sympathy.

The government took fright, and sought an injunction before the B.C. Supreme Court, claiming that further industrial action organized by the unions would be tantamount to sedition as defined in the Criminal Code. Astonishingly, it asserted that not only a general strike, but any "work stoppages, slow-downs, study sessions, breaking and inducing breaches of collective agreements, intimidation, (or) picketing" were to be defined as "the use of force." And no less astonishingly, advocacy of such "use of force" was to be interpreted as "a means of accomplishing a governmental change in the province" insofar as it involved "resisting legislative change, showing Her Majesty has been misled or mistaken in her measures, pointing out errors in the government of the province, procuring alteration in any matter of government, or otherwise interfering with, intimidating or subverting the democratic and constitutional law making process in the Province."[11] That such fascist notions could actually be entertained by a government in Canada indicates how narrow the edge is between democratic and authoritarian capitalism. While hardly questioning the Socreds' fitness to govern by displaying such tendencies, most establishment opinion saw the government's claim as hysterical; and the court pre-emptorily endorsed the unions' request that the action be dismissed.

Despite the government's hysteria, the B.C. Federation had actually rejected the strategy of a general strike to force another election before Bills 19 and 20 were passed. The June 1st strike was a signal of the movement's unity and strength of feeling against the legislation; but this was an adjunct to the Federation's main strategy of boycotting the new Industrial Relation Commission, once the legislation was passed.[12] It was unclear from the beginning whether this strategy was designed to make the new industrial relations regime ineffective by withdrawing all participation in it, and then waiting for an NDP government to eventually repeal it; or for gaining time and preparing the membership for a general strike to support a group of strikers threatened with imprisonment for illegal strike action defined in the new legislation. The two different agendas could not easily be combined. The strategy harkened back to a boycott conducted by the Federation in the late 1960s and early 1970s, against the Mediations Commission Act, when over a dozen leaders and workers went to jail and hundreds of thousands of dollars in fines were levied against the unions before the NDP government, elected in 1972, repealed the Act. (It was reminiscent, as well, of the British TUC's successful strategy against the Heath Government's Industrial Relations Act in the early 1970s.) But key to the earlier boycott's success, as veteran B.C. labour leader, Roy Haynes, recently pointed out, was that the unions

> weren't just avoiding the law or trying to run an end run around it. We were *defying* the law. When they told us to take down our pickets we kept them up. When they ordered us to go back to work we stayed out. And not just when the Commission ordered us. When those same orders were turned into Court decisions, we refused to obey them. We refused to be spooked by the courts.... *The boycott succeeded because union leaders made the conscious decision not to skirt around the laws but to push them to their limits.* They didn't just refuse to obey an order until it was registered in the courts, and then cave in. That gets you nowhere. That doesn't tell the government and employers that you're serious. Caving in before the courts tells them you're *not* serious. Union leaders went to jail because nothing else made the point.[13]

Whatever the Federation leadership's original intentions, the boycott did evolve this way, in practice, in 1987. It was more difficult to effect this because every facet of union entrenchment in the legal framework of recognition and bargaining was now involved. From the beginning, the Federation needed to allow for case-by-case exemptions from the boycott strategy; and before long, it made a general exemption of applications to the Commission for certification of bargaining units. The first case where the new Industrial Relations Commission issued a back-to-work order (against a strike by miners pursuing a first contract, who did not comply with the written strike notice required by the new legislation) and then filed the order before the B.C. Supreme Court, the workers obeyed the order. Moreover, the Federation has in fact tried (unsuccessfully) to skirt the Commission by going to the courts. Although, at this moment, one can only speculate about the way events will evolve, it appears that the momentum of the remarkable June mobilization has been lost; that the new legislation and the Commission will not be rendered inoperative by virtue of the boycott; and the unions will again wait for an NDP victory in the next election, to provide them with the defence they could not muster themselves.

The arguments of those who called for an immediate general strike, to prevent passage of the legislation in the first place, are looking more and more cogent.[14]

Yet, as also needs to be said of the 1983 events, it is questionable whether a general strike itself, if it could be pulled off, amounts to a sufficient strategy. Such a strike, if prolonged, necessarily poses the issue of political power, whatever the intentions of its leaders or participants. Probably, the labour movement could not win such a confrontation in advance of a much more profound education of its own membership, as well as potential allies, regarding the issues at stake. It is not enough to say that, if such a strike leads to the government calling an election, people should vote NDP . The NDP , itself, is embarrassed and defensive about such confrontational struggle; its own message is such as to temper it—if not run from identification with it—rather than make the issues clear. With very few exceptions, this has been the NDP 's orientation, not only in B.C., but right across the country, especially in the face of back-to-work legislation. If there was ever an election in which freedom of association should have stood front and centre in the campaign, it was in September 1984, when upwards of a million workers across the country were still without strike and bargaining rights in the wake of the "6 and 5" measures. Even during the campaign, the right to strike was again removed by back-to-work legislation against urban transit workers in Ontario and B.C. Yet not a murmur was heard from the NDP . Indeed, Ed Broadbent's only reference to "6 and 5" during the famous televised debate among the party leaders was perverse, citing it positively as an example of "target-setting" by governments.

There is probably no way, given the party's base, that the NDP can avoid being associated with class struggles by their political enemies, and indeed, by much of the electorate. Yet, by trying to avoid such identification, the NDP inevitably falls between two stools: it can neither provide a clear perspective on class domination in Canadian society, nor can it escape the charge that it is beholden to the unions; which will continue to be seen by the electorate as a mere "vested interest group," so long as the issue of class struggle is avoided in political discourse. Arthur Scargill's famous admonition to the British Labour Party ("I only wish our leaders were as committed to their class as Mrs. Thatcher is to her's") is relevant here. J.C. Parrot once made a similar point in contrasting Levesque's and Trudeau's electoral style with Broadbent's: "If you had to choose between Trudeau and Broadbent which one are you going to vote for? As the public we don't know too much about politics. But one leader is arguing with you, he is giving you shit, he is telling you what he feels, where he is going, why things are wrong—he is having a debate with you. The other one is trying to find out which side you are on first ... Levesque was elected because he went to the public and said: 'I want to do something different; I've got an alternative and I'm going to fight for it.' He argued with the public, he forced the debate on an issue and suddenly he didn't go down, he went up. A lot of people started to say: 'Well maybe it makes sense.'"[15]

It doesn't always work; nor does such a leader's political fervor usually last, unless there is a mobilized movement pushing the leader from below. Moreover, Mulroney and Vander Zalm being recent examples, it is certainly possible for the leader of a dominant class party to win elections on the basis of a smarmy smile. Eventually perhaps, the NDP 's "Honest Ed" strategy of finding a space within the conventional discourse of Canadian politics, will become credible enough to allow the NDP (at some point) to back into government. But what can it accomplish if it does so on this basis? To return to our original point: such politics are totally incompatible with the kind of class confrontation that a general strike entails. A labour movement that tries to ride two horses at once is, quite simply, going to fall off. One suspects it is because they know this—rather than because they are afraid of the legal consequences—that most labour leaders not only avoid the kind of mobilization a general strike entails, but even avoid mobilizing their members to support strike action in favour of workers directly subject to the state's assault.

It is clear that a new political strategy is needed. But it can hardly be expected that one adequate for the times will emerge without substantial changes occurring in the very character of the labour movement. Does the labour movement understand the actual contours of the new era? And is there any basis for thinking it has the capacity to fashion an appropriate response? Our discussion of the labour movement's unpreparedness for the unfolding of permanent exceptionalism, and its paralysis around the constitutional issues, shows such understanding has not been pronounced. Yet, there is a growing basis for such response to develop, and cautious optimism for its emergence.

Challenges to the ideology of legalism, which has been so immobilizing, are increasing visibly. This is evident in the growing frequency of strikes in outright defiance of laws which ban the right to strike. Strikes like that of NAPE in Newfoundland and of nurses in Alberta in 1988, demonstrate that workers are less and less deferential to abstract invocations of "the rule of law" which uphold specific laws denying fundamental freedoms. The turn toward coercion has itself raised the right to strike to a matter of principle for many workers. Union strategies are, less and less, framed within the parameters of what the law "permits." These challenges to laws that undermine freedom of association as an essential condition of democracy in a capitalist society, with workers prepared to confront the state directly in a determined collective refusal to obey, may yet be the salvation of the right to strike in this country. The fraying of the ideology of legalism can also be seen as workers and union leaders begin questioning how much they ought to depend on legislation to secure their needs. Notable here are: the questioning of FOS in Manitoba; the growing awareness of the centrality of organizing and bargaining in securing material advances for working women, with or without equal pay legislation; the increasing realization by rank-and-file workers that they need to mobilize in their workplaces to secure what health and safety standards ostensibly provide.

None of this can be understood apart from the broad political and cultural changes that are finally affecting the Canadian labour movement. The growing concern with health and safety at the base is related to the spread of environmental concerns in the society. Moreover, union membership is not just composed of recent immigrants (there is nothing unusual about this), but, increasingly, by immigrants of different colours. This makes working-class racism much less external to the union movement than it probably has ever been. The most important change over the last decade, however, is that an increasing number of union members are women; this is no longer news but pertains to the fact that feminism is no longer a movement external to the unions. A growing number of the unions' most committed members and most militant activists are also feminists; and conversely, a growing number of the women involved in feminist struggles are trade unionists. The extent to which the unions have taken up issues like equal pay, day care or sexual harassment, has been in direct response to women organizing for them. Nor are these various developments isolated from one another—indeed, they are intertwined. What appears, at one moment, as a struggle pertaining to immigrant workers, taken up, for instance, via union involvement in English-as-a-second-language programmes, appears again as an issue regarding the specific problems of immigrant women (the double day, sexual harassment, the timing of union meetings, day care). It often reappears as struggles pertaining to health and safety (stress as an occupational hazard, medical screening under the auspices of the union rather than management, etc.).[16]

There is still a broader effect, going beyond conventionally defined "issues." It is notable, and very significant, that the most creative thinking regarding changes in union structures and union politics in Canada in the 1980s, has emerged in the context of the implications of working-class feminism. For instance, sexual harassment is now considered a "legitimate" union issue; but, the problems and possibilities it raises go much deeper, beyond recognition of the "issue" itself. As Heather Maroney has put it:

> In the labour force, sexual harassment strengthens both vertical hierarchy and horizontal divisions to maintain women in their traditional inferior position.... The net result is to reinforce male solidarity across class lines, to blur class divisions through working-class sexism, to fragment, the solidarity of a working class that has two sexes, and to reinforce class domination. How this issue is resolved depends in large part on political choices made by working -class feminists. Union officials are likely to try to contain some of its more radical elements on the understandable grounds that unions are, after all, organizations for economic defence and not for liberation struggles. Opening up the full dimensions of this question may indeed initially be "divisive," if not on the convention floor then on the shop floor. But the full exploration of this issue holds the potential to strengthen unions. Even in the short-run, active educational campaigns under the control of rank-and-file women would increase their participation and provide them with the political experience and clout necessary to occupy other leadership positions. An understanding of the full implications of this issue *at all levels* of the unions would be an important step in carrying out in the medium term the ideological and organizational reforms that are needed to correspond to the increase in female membership. [17]

The implications of this can be taken further still. For women to debate and develop tactics and strategy in separate women's committees and conferences, even the creation of elected positions reserved for women, as a means of lessening male dominance in leadership positions, has created, as Linda Briskin has pointed out, "a whole new level of debate around the elections." This raises questions not only about "What do women represent?" and "What kind of women do we want?" but also about "What are the politics of this?" Resistance to women organizing separately in the unions, and women's confrontation of this, as Briskin notes, brings important implications for overcoming the resistance among union leaderships to

> rank and file organizing in general ... to more democracy, to more rank and file input, to more militancy.... It's been difficult for women to organize because it's been difficult for most people to organize inside unions, and we have to see some of the problems of women organizing within the unions as symptomatic of larger problems with apathy and so on. We have to look for structures to encourage more participation and to fight against apathy.... [18]

The effects of feminism, health and safety concerns, and the changing composition of union membership, create strong, and very broad, new tensions within the labour movement as old practices are challenged. These tensions are often, it must be admitted, only responded to by unions in a hit-and-miss way. But it is also important to recognize that the tensions themselves both arise out of and contribute to a changing pattern of union struggles, of a kind perhaps not seen since the 1930s. The way campaigns for unionization in the retail and banking sectors, where struggles by women keep bubbling up again and again in the 1980s, in the very face of the difficult organizing conditions and implacable capitalist resistance, bespeak a new tenaciousness. We have already mentioned the nurses' strike in Alberta which suggests the same thing. This is hardly confined to women, as the Gainers strike and the recent recognition strikes by construction workers in that province indicate. Even the realization that collective bargaining can't secure the same kinds of monetary wage gains it did in the era of free collective bargaining and post-war boom, seems to be producing a capacity to struggle around other issues that go well beyond just holding on to what you have. The preparedness of young workers to take strike action for pension indexing is one example; but, recent mobilizations around health and safety are more telling. Rank-and-file workers have been pushing both their union leaders and the state into action, often by taking direct action themselves. Workers are using the state, but in a different manner than through the procedural framework collective bargaining legislation provides. They are using—or demanding—state criteria on adequate health and safety while recognizing that these criteria are only enforceable in a mobilized union environment.

A similar logic underlies the recent splits by Canadian sections from their American "international parents," the most visible development in the changing character of the union movement. If growing nationalism has aided this, it has been far from determinant; nor has a narrow economism been determinant, either. The splits have often been on the principled grounds of resisting corporate strategies that threaten workers and the integrity of their organizations, especially on the shop floor, through the individualism and competition inherent in profit-sharing schemes. The declaration of independence by the Autoworkers is widely recognized as historic; but the actual salience of this and recent similar developments already profoundly affecting Canadian politics, is often enough not spelled out clearly.

The north-south orientation of "international" unionism was a powerful impetus to sectionalism and fragmentation in the Canadian labour movement. This orientation was the basis of the unions' endorsement of Canada's neo-colonial relationship with the United States and the pattern of continental capitalist accumulation in the post-war period. The obvious dissonance between the labour movement today and the free trade thrust of capital and the state is the result of the historic break with this orientation. Not unrelated is the fact that anti-communism has had a sharply declining purchase on working-class conscious-ness in Canada. Consequently, fewer and fewer labour leaders have been willing (or at least able) to play this card with the membership. In the United States, nationalist identification was connected to the displacing of the class struggle to the international conflict between communism and "Americanism." A growing nationalist feeling in the Canadian labour movement has been accompanied, not only with a greater awareness of the nature of American imperialism, but also with support for many internationalist (and some domestic) struggles, in which communists are visible actors. The newly Canadianized unions have, necessar-ily, had to move toward forging horizontal alliances; not just through mergers and common action with other unions, but through developing linkages with other progressive social forces. In many unions, the struggle to separate has also raised to the fore the issue of greater internal democracy. This has important imp-lications, not only for changes in individual union structures, but also for changes at the level of the provincial federations and the CLC, as we shall shortly see.

However important all these changes have been, we must still be mindful of their limits, in terms both of ideology and structure. Ideologically, the labour movement is still largely enveloped in an understanding which tends to reduce the state to the government of the day, and fails to see the state as a constituent element of capitalist domination. Struggles continued to be framed within the parameters of actually-existing capitalism and the actually-existing state. This can be seen in the campaign against free trade that has gathered round the labour movement. The broadly-based alliance strategy, which reflects a new openness to social movements and a new understanding of the curse of continentalism, is admirably conjoined to a discourse posing the issue in terms of "big business versus the people." At the same time, and despite all the evidence to which this study attests, there is a persistent glorification of the beneficent nature of the Canadian state—the constant invocations to decency and democracy as the leitmotifs of the Canadian welfare state. Only Mulroney's abject tailing of Reaganism appears as an exception. Against free trade, no vision other than one of managing capitalism better—a revitalized Keynesian welfare state, more Canadian ownership, trade diversification—is advanced. Job security is really the main focus of labour's concerns. Undeniably important as this is, it still reflects a lingering economism. Finally, reminiscent of Dennis McDermott's reduction of the issues of the 1984 election to Trudeau's "obscene immorality," the impression created is that defeating the Mulroney government is the key unlocking the door to a secure future—a negative and defensive posture rather than a positive and challenging one.

This limited perspective hardly applies to all activist or even all leadership elements in the movement. But, almost all employ a discourse consistent with it. This partially reflects a legitimate and understandable defensiveness, a desire to retain whatever collective rights possible in the face of the capitalist offensive, and to mobilize the resources and support available to do so. It also reflects their understanding that to do more, it would be necessary to undertake the daunting task of changing the parameters of Canadian politics. Admittedly, existing union structures are not well-suited to the task. However, defensiveness is no longer enough.

Collective bargaining can't achieve the gains it once did. Even an NDP government standing on its own can't secure the needs, let alone the aspirations, of working people in this period of international capitalist competition and restructuring. Labour movement recognition that the political environment must be changed seems to be growing, but there is a certain reluctance to draw the conclusion that flows from this. The most significant aspect of a changing political environment is a change in the consciousness of working people. In the boom days of the post-war era and rising welfare state, when the focus of the struggle was on negotiating wage increases, it mattered less what the ideological dispositions of workers were. Today, it matters a great deal: changing the political environment has to begin and be sustained by a strong popular commitment to challenging the limits of actually-existing capitalism and the actually-existing state.

How can unions change to forge such a commitment? Union strategies and structures along at least three crucial dimensions would seem necessary. Firstly, the union movement needs to become much more political. We don't mean by this just making demands upon the state, or identifying with a political party and supporting it electorally; we mean being much more political *vis-à-vis* their membership. The problem is not that the unions are oriented toward defeating free trade or electing the NDP. The problem is leaving politics *at that* . Not enough attention is given to the process of political education, upwards and downwards in the labour movement, in relation to the broad complex of social relations that touch on workers' lives. Ultimately, it is upon this and the mobilization that can be built on it that the unions' capacity to affect the state depends.

Secondly, unions will have to become much more open, democratic and flexible than most of them currently are. Too often, solidarity within union structures—conceived primarily as loyalty to the leadership—is purchased at the cost of internal democracy. Union leaders' assertions to employers that they should engage in serious bargaining, because they control the rank and file, is inadequate in the face of the present capitalist offensive. The goal must be the creation of the most openly democratic procedures, affording members the opportunity and resources to make effective decisions at all levels of the union. It must be said that the unions in Canada, as elsewhere, have seldom come close to this; nor has their post-war envelopment in the legal framework been a salutary influence. It exacerbated the hierarchical development within unions; appointed officials, with technical skills and enormous powers of control over the direction of the union, all too often had little inclination or means of dialogue with the membership. This structure is not just related to centralization in union organizations; indeed, the legal framework of certification and bargaining—put on a local by local, employer *cum* workplace basis—fragments unions, weakening the basis for member participation and control over elected and appointed officials. The Rand formula, arguably the most important state sanction in favour of union solidarity, paradoxically loosened the link, so crucial to securing union recognition, between union finances and membership commitment.

In the infamous *Lavigne* case against OPSEU in Ontario, the National Citizens' Coalition, a right-wing lobby led by major sectors of financial capital, orchestrated and financed an attempt to challenge the Rand formula under the Charter.[19] The objective was to uncouple the dues check-off provision's guarantee of funds for the unions' collective bargaining activities from their political activities. Lavigne felt the dues check-off clause, legitimated by the Rand formula, meant that he was not only financing collective bargaining but also any political causes the union supported, thereby being deprived of his freedom of association by paying for causes he did not wish to support. The NCC understood full well the importance of the political dimension of trade unionism we have been discussing, and, no less well, just how thin the politicization of the membership actually is. In the event, the union got off lightly. The trial judge ruled that the Rand formula did infringe the freedom of association of the individual, but that this was a reasonable limit, under section 1 of the Charter, since expenditures were related to the preserving and enhancing of collective bargaining. He subsequently drew a liberal line encompassing most political expenditures and required dissenters to go to the trouble of explicitly opting out of the "political" portion of their dues. Such challenges will not go away; the danger is that in so far as the unions ward off challenges by minimizing the scope and significance of their political activities, the NCC and their ilk win a substantive victory whatever the court decisions. Reliance on the Rand formula and other legal devices is simply inadequate and, ultimately, unprincipled. The only way the unions can win this game is by politicizing as many of their members as possible.

The legal framework by which a particular union wins exclusive bargaining rights has also sustained a proprietary notion of membership on the part of union leaders. This imposes on labour federations, particularly the CLC, the unending and unsavory task of mediating jurisdictional disputes amongst their affiliates. It is almost impossible for union members appealing to central labour movement structures to secure democratization of their unions or retain federation affiliation if they move to form new ones. One of the consequences of the recent splits from the Internationals has been to call into question this state of affairs. Much of the appeal of Canadianization relates to the issue of union democracy, and has encouraged a process of organization and mergers; this has pressured the CLC to concern itself with more than just formal autonomy declarations by Canadian sections of Internationals, and extend its concerns to how democratic individual union structures really are—hardly just a problem with the international union structures. For their part, activists aware of the importance of democratic procedures, and sensitive to their abuse, all too often fail to pursue the issue, frequently confusing solidarity with democracy. Even in the case of the most blatant authoritarianism and/or corruption—as in many construction trades—little support is given to those trying to democratize their unions. But, there are increasing dangers associated with the perpetuation of the existing situation. Ongoing state intervention in union affairs coincides with growing demand by union members for internal democracy; the danger is that the latter will be used to justify the former. Unless labour centrals take up the question of internal union democracy, the state may well step in—with potentially great costs to the legitimacy of the unions, and the significant possibility of further inroads on freedom of association.

Democratization is directly related to the possibilities of politicization, as already suggested; but it is also crucial for a further kind of change the movement requires today. Enhanced democratic structures can contribute to a more committed and involved membership, opening the way for unions to become, as far as possible, centres of working-class life and culture. In the final analysis, this development alone can root the labour movement in the society. Union activists and leaders must engage directly—not just as surrogates issuing statements which favour issues taken up by the social movements so important today—in the many spheres of working peoples' lives. They should not only struggle for new and broader benefits and services in collective agreements and legislation, but also actively involve communities in the issues that affect them—from housing, to transport, to education, to racism and sexism. It is not enough to win for workers more "leisure" via reduced work-time: there will have to be a concern with working people when they are not at work, and that includes part-timers and those unemployed. The unions must investigate non-market means to satisfy the human need to be productive and creative in and out of work, the need for more than the compensation of indebted consumption in return for the lack of control over work, as well as over the economy and the state.

The labour movement has to become the vehicle through which working people develop confidence in their capacity to lead society. The working class mobilization and struggle that launched the era of free collective bargaining grew out of an earlier capitalist crisis, and an earlier confrontation with reactionary forces. But, a much broader political project which deeply infused the labour movement was the socialist purpose at the time, inspiring and sustaining labour struggles to a significant degree. It is inconceivable that the necessary changes in the labour movement could occur apart from a revitalization of that purpose. This means taking risks among members, who, often enough, don't see the connection between their immediate reasons for joining or supporting unions and the struggle against capitalism as a system. But the risk can no longer be avoided. The unions must provide their members with a sense that they can realize a socialist alternative to actually-existing capitalism and the actually-existing state, and, at the same time, become centres for broader public education in this regard. To be sure, this will mean educating those leaders who cannot see beyond defensiveness and economism and still hope falsely for an easy return to full union rights and the expansive Keynesian welfare state; and educating a membership who have rarely been given the opportunity to learn how capitalism works as a system; who have only been exposed to the most caricatured or impoverished notions of socialism, rather than the new possibilities for workers' creativity and self-determination it could open. If the lessons drawn from the continuing assault on union freedoms combine with the effusive tensions within unions today in such a way as to imbue the labour movement with a socialist purpose and practices, the 1980s may yet be seen as having laid the basis for the advance of the Canadian working class.

Finally, one thing must be stressed above all: freedom of association for workers is an essential condition of democracy. Achieved through long, arduous, even bloody, struggle, it was only accepted by the state at real cost to the further mobilizing capacities of unions. Moreover, it was always, in a capitalist society, open to challenge. Reforms, even reforms basic to liberal democracy, are always subject to limits and never guaranteed forever. They must be defended, extended and transformed to further strengthen workers' capacity to conduct class struggle—or else they are always in danger of atrophying, or worse, being reneged. The struggle to defend workers' freedom of association in Canada today, is a struggle over the substantive meaning of democracy in a capitalist society. If the labour movement loses that struggle, it also loses the autonomy from the state and capital that gives the labour movement its capacity to reform and, ultimately, to transform society.

Notes

Chapter 1

1. Q. Hoare and G. Nowell Smith, ed. and trans., *Selections from the Prison Notebooks of Antonio Gramsci*, (London: Laurence and Wishart, 1971), pp. 246-7.
2. Quoted in *The Weekend Evening Telegram*, St. John's, October 25, 1986.
3. M. Thompson and A. Ponak, "Canadian Public Sector Industrial Relations: Policy and Practice," a paper delivered at the Pacific Rim Comparative Labour Policy Conference, Vancouver, 1987, pp. 31,41.
4. P. Kumar, "Recent Labour-Management Approaches in Canada: Will They Endure?" (Kingston: Queen's Papers in Industrial Relations, 1987) p.4.
5. D. Carter, "The Changing Face of Canadian Labour Relations Law," Working Paper no. 54, (Kingston: Industrial Relations Centre, Queen's University, 1985) p. 13.

Chapter 2

1. Hal Draper, *Karl Marx's Theory of Revolution, Volume II: The Politics of Social Classes*, (New York: Monthly Review Press, 1973) p. 234.
2. See Claude D'Aoust and François Delorme, "The Origins of the Freedom of Association and of the Right of Strike in Canada: An Historical Perspective," *Relations Industrielles* 36:4, 1981, pp. 894-919.3.
3. Paul Craven, "An Impartial Umpire," *Industrial Relations and the Canadian State 1900-1911* (Toronto: University of Toronto Press, 1980), p. 306. Craven notes (cf. pp. 301-302) that H.D. Woods, despite arguing that the primary purpose of the IDIA was "the establishment of a bargaining relationship, and not, as commonly supposed, the delaying of strikes or lockouts," concludes that in practice it "was little more than a public-interest emergency-dispute policy."

4. Justice I.C. Rand, "Rand Formula," *Canadian Law Reports*, 2150 (1958), pp. 1251-1253.

5. H.A. Logan, *State Intervention and Assistance in Collective Bargaining* (Toronto: University of Toronto Press, 1956), p. 75.

6. L. Sefton-MacDowell, "The Formation of the Canadian Industrial Relations System During World War Two," *Labour/Le Travailleur* (1978), pp. 175-196.

7. Logan, op. cit. p. 76

8. For a survey of the relevant literature, see L. Panitch, "Elites, Class and Power in Canada," in M.S. Whittington and G. Williams (eds.), *Canadian Politics in the 1980's* (Toronto: Methuen, 1981), 2nd Edition, pp. 229-251.

9. H. Laski, *Trade Unions in the New Society* (London: George Allen and Unwin, 1950), pp. 66-67.

10. Ibid., pp. 224, 232.

11. Paul Weiler, *Reconcilable Differences: New Directions in Canadian Labour Law* (Toronto: Carswell, 1980).

12. H.A. Logan, op cit., pp. 26, 27. The "formal" equality of the ban on strikes and lockouts during collective agreements is, needless to say, illusory since the lockout is but one of several of capital's economic weapons.

13. Rand, op. cit., p. 1252.

14. D. Swartz, "The Politics of Reform: Conflict and Accommodation in Canadian Health Policy," in L. Panitch (ed.), *The Canadian State: Political Economy and Political Power*, (Toronto: University of Toronto Press, 1977), pp. 311-343. Immediate post-war reforms were often presented as "down payments" toward more comprehensive measures. For example, federal assistance to the provinces for extending health facilities particularly hospitals, was presented as a step toward health insurance—a Liberal party "promise" since 1919.

15. It is well recognized that the working conditions (including pay and managerial practices) of public employees were inferior to those of private sector workers employed by major corporations. It should be noted here that in 1944 the CCF government in Saskatchewan granted bargaining rights to provincial employees.

16. S. Jamieson, *Industrial Relations in Canada* (Toronto: MacMillan, 1973), 130 ff. The unionized proportion of the workforce did "jump" from 30 to 33 per cent between 1952-1953, and then slowly declined to just below 30 per cent in the mid-1960s. The 1952-1953 increase was due primarily to a contraction of one hundred thousand in the labour force. In British Columbia, new restrictions were imposed on the right to strike generally, while in Alberta, what were deemed "public interest disputes" were subject to more sweeping restrictions.

17. This position was common on the "left" as well as in the mainstream thinking. For example, see H. Marcuse, *One Dimensional Man* (Boston: Beacon Press, 1964) and J. O'Connor, *The Fiscal Crisis of the State* (New York: St. Martin's Press, 1973)

18. R. Miliband, *The State in Capitalist Society* (New York: Basic Books, 1969), p. 217.

19. S. Jamieson, op. cit., pp. 94-99.

20. For a good overview, see K. McRoberts and D. Postgate, *Quebec: Social Change and Political Crisis*, rev. ed. (Toronto: McClelland and Stewart, 1980).

21. H. Arthurs, *Collective Bargaining by Public Employees in Canada: The Five Models*, (Ann Arbor: Institute of Labour and Industrial Relations, 1971).

22. There has been some suggestion that Jean Marchand, the former President of the Confederation of National Trade Unions (CSN) and the most sought after of the "three wise men," made granting the right to strike a condition for remaining in the government. (Personal communication from E. Swimmer.)

23. S. Goldenberg, "Collective Bargaining in the Provincial Public Services," in *Collective Bargaining in the Public Service* (Toronto: The Institute of Public Administration of Canada, 1973). This useful, if somewhat dated, overview of provincial labour legislation may now be supplemented by Goldenberg's major study with J. Finkelman, *Collective Bargaining in the Public Service: The Federal Experience in Canada*, (Montreal: The Institute for Research on Public Policy, 1983), esp. vol. I, Ch. 1

24. David Lewis, *The Good Fight: Political Memoirs 1909-1958,* (Toronto: Macmillan, 1981), p. 393.
25. Ibid., p. 151.26.H. Logan, op. cit., p. 76.
27. C. Offe and H. Wiesenthal, "Two Logics of Collective Action," *Political Power and Social Theory,* 1 (1979).
28. For a brilliant elaboration of this argument in the context of the United States, see K. Klare, "Jurisdicial Deradicalization of the Wagner Act and the Origins of Modern Legal Consciousness 1937-1974," *Minnesota Law Review,* 62 (1978), pp. 265-339. R. Warskett in "Trade Unions in the Canadian State: A Case Study of Bank Worker Unionization 1976-1980," M.A. Thesis (Carleton University, 1981), develops a similar argument in her timely and insightful study of efforts to organize bank workers in Canada.
29. For a graphic illustration see J. Deverell, "The Ontario Hospital Dispute 1980-1981," *Studies in Political Economy: A Socialist Review,* 9 (1982), pp. 179-190.

Chapter 3

1. P.E. Trudeau, *The Asbestos Strike* (1956), James Boake (tr.), (Toronto: James Lewis and Samuel, 1974), p. 336.
2. See E. Swimmer, "Militancy in Public Sector Unions," in M. Thompson and E. Swimmer (eds.), *Conflict or Compromise: Public Sector Industrial Relations in Canada* (The Institute for Research on Public Policy, 1984).
3. This boom was, in fact, the product of the historically specific set of conditions at the end of World War II: the unchallenged dominance of the United States *vis-à-vis* the major capitalist countries which allowed it to order the international financial system; the extensive task of post-war reconstruction in Europe; discoveries of huge cheap resources; the colonial or neo-colonial dependency of most of the Third World, and the moderation of the labour movement in the West, not least due to the Cold War. While signs of their passing were already dimly visible by the mid-sixties, the "formal announcement" came in 1971, when United States President Nixon renounced the Breton Woods Agreement on which the post-war international financial order was based. See, for example, I. Gough, "State Expenditure in Advanced Capitalism," *New Left Review,* Number 92, July/August 1975.
4. See, for example, D. Wolfe, "The State and Economic Policy in Canada 1968-1975," in L. Panitch (ed.), *Canadian State,* pp. 228-251 and I. Gillespie, "On the Redistribution of Income in Canada," *Canadian Tax Journal,* 24 (July/August 1976), pp. 419-450.
5. See L. Panitch, "The Development of Corporatism in Liberal Democracies," *Comparative Political Studies,* 10 (April 1977), pp. 61-90.
6. A discussion of these attempts in Canada and the reasons for their failure is found in L. Panitch, "Corporatism in Canada?" *Studies in Political Economy: A Socialist Review* 1 (Spring 1979), pp. 43-92. See also A. Maslove and E. Swimmer, *Wage Controls in Canada 1975-1978,* (Montreal: The Institute for Research on Public Policy, 1980).
7. Quoted in A. Price, "Back to Work Legislation: An Analysis of the Federal and Ontario Governments' Increased Propensity to End Strikes by Ad Hoc Laws, 1950-1978," M.A. Thesis, (Kingston: Queen's University, 1980), p. 98. Price concludes that seldom, if ever, was there such a threat. Rather, government intervention was designed to prevent serious disruption of immediate concern to a relatively small segment of society, or to prevent broad public inconvenience (p. 90).
8. Ibid., p. 99.
9. This table has largely been constructed from "Emergency Legislation and Orders Suspending the Right to Strike or to Lock Out," Federal-Provincial Relations,

Labour Canada, 1987, as checked and supplemented by our own search of Labour Canada's *Legislative Review*. Note that the figures include 82 instances of back-to-work Acts and 18 instances of suspensions of the right to strike by Order-in-Council under the Industrial Relations Acts of Alberta (7 from 1971 to 1980) and new Brunswick (4 from 1979 to 1985), under the Quebec Labour Code as amended in 1982 (3 in 1986-87) and under the British Columbia Essential Services Disputes Act (4 in 1985-86). See Appendix I for a complete list of the measures since 1950.

10. H.J. Glasbeek and M. Mandel, "The Crime and Punishment of Jean-Claude Parrot," *Canadian Forum* (August 1979), pp. 10-14.
11. Quoted in L. Panitch, *Workers, Wages and Controls: The Anti-Inflation Programme and its Implications for Canadian Workers,* (Toronto: New Hogtown Press, 1976), especially pp. 1 and 18.
12. Quoted in *The Globe and Mail*, October 21, 1982.
13. For a cogent alternative view of the "6 and 5" legislation which mainly sees it as an attempt to renege on the collective bargaining rights granted to federal government employees, see E. Swimmer, "Six and Five," in A. Maslove (ed.), *How Ottawa Spends 1984*, pp. 240-281. While not disputing the specifics of his argument, the ensuing course of events seems to us to confirm the significance of the broader ideological factors we identify as being involved.
14. Quoted in *The Globe and Mail*, October 21, 1982.
15. P. Weiler, *Reconcilable Differences* (Toronto: 1980), p. 254.
16. The following account is essentially based upon an analysis of the actual Legislative Record. A basic overview can be obtained from two Labour Canada, serial publications: *Legislative Review*, no 16, June 1983 (annual) plus Monthly Updates, nos. 55-63; and *Collective Bargaining Review*, 1984, nos 1-3. The following publications, in addition to those cited in the text, were also particularly useful: Canadian Union of Public Employees, *The Facts*, vol. 5, no. 4, May 1983 and vol. 5, no. 6, July/August 1983; the British Columbia Government Employees Union *Bulletin*, no. 7, 8 August 1983 (on the British Columbia government's package of legislation accompanying its budget); R. Sass, "An Assessment of the Saskatchewan Trade Union Amendment Act, 1983," *Saskatchewan Law Review*, vol. 48, no. 1, 1983-84; and G. Makahonuk, "The Trade Union Act (Saskatchewan) is Under Attack," *Briarpatch*, vol. 12:3, April 1983.
17. See "The Turning Point in Industrial Relations" and "Government Moves to Restrain Construction Wages," *Construction*, 19:3, September/October 1983, pp. 3-4 and pp. 17-19.
18. The "designation" of the Governor General's gardener during the 1974 strike by the general labour and trades group illustrates the willingness of the government to exploit this provision.
19. *The Canadian Air Traffic Control Asociation versus the Treasury Board*, May 31, 1982.
20. B. Fleming, "Memorandum to Education Officers," February 14, 1985, Public Service Alliance of Canada.
21. In what *The Globe and Mail* termed a "radical decision," Compensation Commissioner Ed Peck confirmed on March 14, 1984 the government's "ability to pay" as the paramount consideration, and not a "fair wage," in overturning a binding arbitration award of five per cent to school support staff workers. Once the government set funding levels, collective bargaining had to take place within those parameters. See *The Globe and Mail*, 15 March 1984.
22. The following account is based on B. Palmer, "A Funny Thing Happened on the Way to Kelowna," in *Canadian Dimension* 18:1, March 1984, p. 6; and L. Kuehn, "B.C. Teachers Strengthen the Labour Movement," in *Canadian Dimension* 18:01, March 1984, pp. 9-12.
23. *The Globe and Mail*, March 19, 1984.
24. B. Livingstone, "Alberta Labour Under Attack," *Canadian Dimension*, 18:2, May 1984, pp. 21-22. See also *The Globe and Mail*, July 3, 1984, for a report updating this issue in view of subsequent board rulings.

Chapter 4

1. Letter to Conrad Schmidt, in R. Tucker (ed.), *The Marx-Engels Reader*, (New York: W.W. Norton, 1972), pp. 645-6. Harry Glasbeek offers the most insightful work in Canadian labour law from this perspective: see most recently his "Law; Real and Ideological Constraints on the Working Class," in D. Gibson and T.R. Baldwin (eds.), *Law in a Cynical Society*, (Calgary/Vancouver: Carswell, 1985), pp. 282-301; and more specifically, his "Voluntarism, Liberalism, and Grievance Arbitration: Holy Grail, Romance and Real Life," in G. England (ed.) *Government and Labour Relations: The Death of Voluntarism*, (Toronto: CCH, 1986), esp. pp. 59-66.
2. This table is derived from Table 2 of I.U. Zeytinoglou, "The ILO Standards and Canadian Labour Legislation," *Relations Industrielles*, Vol. 42, no. 2, 1987, p. 301.
3. ILO, *Official Bulletin, Reports of the Committee on Freedom of Association*, Vol. LXV, (Geneva: 1982), Series B, no. 2, pp. 149-71; cf. Special Supplement, Vol. LXVII, 1984.
4. *Official Bulletin*, Vol. LXIII, 1980, pp. 45-51.
5. For an overview of ILO rulings on Alberta, see *Official Bulletin*, Vol. LXVIII, Series B, no. 3, 1985, esp. pp. 34-5.
6. *Official Bulletin*, Vol. LXIV, 1981, pp. 5-10, and Vol. LXVI, 1983, pp. 24-34.
7. This summary draws on Zeytinoglou, op. cit., but see also "International Labour Organization's Committee on Freedom of Association Conclusions (November 1985) in Cases Relating to Canada," *Collective Bargaining Review*, December 1985, pp. 133-35; and "ILO Condemns Labour Laws in Canada," *Canadian Labour*, January 1986, pp. 12-15.
8. Quoted in Zeytinoglou, p. 304.
9. *Re Service Employees International Union, Local 204 and Broadway Manor Nursing Home* (1983), 4 D.L.R. (4th) 231 (Ont. Div. Ct.), affirmed on other grounds (1984), 13 D.L.R. (4th) 220 (Ont. C.A.).
10. *Re Public Service Employees Act, Labour Relations Act and Police Officers Collective Bargaining Act* (1984) 16 D.L.R. (4th) 359 (Alta. C.A.).
11. *Black vs. Law Society of Alberta* (1986) 3 W.W.R. 590 (Alta. C.A.).
12. See *Public Service Alliance of Canada v. The Queen* (1984) 2 F.C. 889, and Trial Division (1984) 2 F.C. 562, 11 D.L.R. (4th) 337, 9, C.R.R. 248.
13. *Dolphin Delivery Ltd. v. Retail, Wholesale and Department Store Union, Local 580*, (1984), 10 D.L.R. (4th) 198 (B.C. C.A.).
14. See *Re Prime and Manitoba Labour Board* (1983), 3 D.L.R. (4th) 74 (Man. Q.B.); *Halifax Police Officers and NCOs Association v. City of Halifax* (1984), 11 C.L.R. 358 (S.C.N.S.T.D.); and *Newfoundland Association of Public Employees v. The Queen* (1985), 14 C.R.R. 193 (Nfld. S.C.T.D.).
15. See the Appeal Court review reference in n. 5 above, and also Lorne Slotnick, "Appeal Court Sidesteps Charter in Ruling on Restraint Law," *The Globe and Mail*, October 23, 1984.
16. *Re Retail, Wholesale and Department Store Union, Locals 544, 496, 635 and 955 and Government of Saskatchewan* (1985), 19 D.L.R. (4th) 609 (Sask. C.A.).
17. The SGEU Dispute Settlement Act, Bill 144, January 31, 1986.
18. The following discussion and the quotations and references pertaining thereto are drawn from: *Reference re Public Service Employment Relations Act* (Alta.) (1987), 1 S.C.R., pp. 313-423; *PSAC v. Canada* (1987), 1 S.C.R., pp. 424-459; and *RWDSU v. Saskatchewan* (1987), 1 S.C.R., pp. 460-496, all dated April 9, 1987.
19. See C. D'Aoust and F. Delorme, "The origins of the Freedom of Association and the Right to Strike in Canada: An Historical Perspective," *Relations Industrielles*, Vol. 36, No. 4, 1981, esp. pp. 908-9.
20. See note 18, above.
21. Ibid.
22. Ibid.

23. Ibid.
24. Ibid.
25. "Labour law won't change after ruling, expert says," *The Toronto Star*, April 13, 1987.
26. The quotations are in Patricia Poirier, "Court dashes labour hopes of more rights," *The Globe and Mail*, April 10, 1987.
27. Harry Arthurs, quoted in "University Head sees new industrial relations climate," *The Globe and Mail*, February 28, 1985. Cf. his "The Right to Golf: Reflections on the Future of Workers, Unions and the Rest of Us under the Charter," Address to the "Labour Law Under the Charter" Conference, Industrial Relations Centre, Queen's University, Sept. 24, 1987. A very different, albeit rather naive, view of the benefits to be had from the charter for individual workers' rights, is provided by Prof. David M. Beatty, in *Putting the Charter to Work*, (Kingston/Montreal: McGill/Queen's, 1987).

Chapter 5

1. "Recent Labour-Management Approaches in Canada: Will They Endure?" (Kingston: Queen's Papers in Industrial Relations, 1987), p. 4.
2. Editorial, *The Globe and Mail*, October 8, 1982.
3. *Reference re: Public Service Employees Relations Act* (Alta.), S.C.C. No. 19234, April 9, 1987, p. 40.
4. See J. Deverell, "CLC Chief's Obsession Puts NDP in Peril," *The Toronto Star*, February 12, 1984.
5. See G. Sulzner, "Canadian Federal Labour-Management Relations: The Mulroney Difference," *Journal of Collective Negotiations in the Public Sector*, Vol. 15 (4), 1986, esp. pp. 294-5; B. Estabrook, "Labour Seeks Role in Tory Economic Planning," *Financial Times*, November 19, 1984.
6. *Hansard*, November 18, 1986, p. 1265.
7. Quoted in J. Deverell, "Ottawa Pushing 100,000 Workers into Strike Action Union Leaders Say," *The Toronto Star*, April 4, 1987.
8. See *Hansard*, August 27, 1987, pp. 8482-8525.
9. *Hansard*, ibid. This pattern, needless to say, was equally evident in the case of the back-to-work legislation imposed on CUPW, as we shall see shortly.
10. Quoted in *The Globe and Mail*, August 28, 1987.
11. See J. Deverell, "End Strike and Back Post Office Business Group Urges," *The Toronto Star*, October 6, 1987.
12. Quoted in J. Deverell, "Ottawa May Use Closure to End Strike by Posties," *The Toronto Star*, October 14, 1987.
13. Interview by Michael Enright with Harvie André on CBC's "As It Happens," October 8, 1987. The inclusion of this sanction in the legislation, ending the lockout of longshoremen in Vancouver, very much caught the attention of liberal M.P. Sheila Copps (*Hansard*, November 18, 1987, p. 1258). However, outside of her intervention in the House of Commons, it generated little comment.
14. The greater number of entries in Table V than in Table IV reflects the fact that all bargaining units have now "negotiated" a post-controls collective agreement. Any discrepencies in the level of designations for bargaining units in both tables is due to the fact that a) the entries in Table IV are the number of designations the Treasury Board initially proposed to the PSSRB (and which it may have agreed to alter, in light of union representations), whereas those in Table V are the number of positions actually designated; or b) the entries in Table IV refer to an earlier round of negotiations than those in Table V.
15. G. Sulzner, "Canadian Federal Labour-Management Relations: The Mulroney Difference," *Journal of Collective Negotiations*, 1986, 15:4, p. 298. See also Wilfred List, "Crew's Dilemma Raises the Issue of the Right to Strike," *The Globe and Mail*, July 7, 1986.

16. Taken from G. Swimmer, "Changes to Public Service Labour Relations Legislation: Revitalizing or Destroying Collective Bargaining?" in M. Prince (ed.), *How Ottawa Spends 1987-88: Restraining the State*, (Ottawa: Methuen, 1987), pp. 313-14.

17. "Federal Unions Angry at Plans to Amend Act," *The Globe and Mail*, January 14, 1987. This opinion, coming from the union's architect of the deal abandoning the right to strike over the Master Agreement, should be taken with a grain of salt. It's not at all clear that much scope for collective bargaining remains under present levels of designations or that the current PSSRA is in any way a barrier to increasing them.

18. G. Swimmer, "The Impact of the Dispute Settlement Process on Canadian Federal Public Service Wage Settlements," *Journal of Collective Negotiations*, 1987, 16:1, pp. 53-61.

19. M. Lim, "An Overview of Recent Compensation Settlements in the Canadian Public Sector," *Proceedings*, Canadian Compensation Association Conference, 1985, pp. 35-39.

20. See V. Bercovici, "Loss of Wage Schedule Helps Non-union Firms, Say Unions," *The Ottawa Citizen*, July 30, 1987.

21. In the welter of temporary legislation affecting public sector workers during the controls period, this important expansion of the executive powers of the state went unnoticed, including by ourselves.

22. L. Slotnick, "Proposed Bill Seeks to Curb Power of B.C.'s Labour Unions," *The Globe and Mail*, May 11, 1987.

23. Business Council of British Columbia, *B.C. Collective Bargaining Review and Outlook*, 1985, p. 24.

24. Following the 1984 revisions, certifications of new bargaining units fell from 441 in 1983 to 238 in 1984. Decertifications rose markedly, especially in the construction industry. See *The Globe and Mail*, July 15, 1985.

25. *B.C. Collective Bargaining Review and Outlook*, op. cit. A good example of this trend was the "very tough deal" agreed to by workers in the forest industry. See R. Lester, "Causes and Effects of De-Accreditation on Collective Bargaining in the British Columbia Pulp and Paper Industry," *Proceedings*, 23rd Annual Meeting of the Industrial Relations Association, University of Manitoba, May 29-31, 1986, p. 380.

26. D. Forkin, "IWA Defeats Contracting-Out," *Our Times*, February 1987, p. 12-13.

27. "Open Letter to the Premier," *The Province*, May 31, 1987. On the centralization effected by Vander Zalm, see J. Cruickshank, "Vander Zalm Runs a One-Man Show to Speed Reforms," *The Globe and Mail*, July 15, 1987.

28. The implications of Bill 19, particularly regarding women workers, are incisively and wittily analysed by Sharon Yandle in "The Women at Windermere," *New Directions*, Vol. 2 (5), June 1987, p. 3-6.

29. See ILO *Official Bulletin*, Vol. LXIX, 1986, Series B., No. 1, pp. 40-48.

30. "Continuing the Furor over Labour," *Western Report*, August 17, 1987.

31. L. Slotnick, "Proposed Bill Seeks to Curb Powers of B.C. Labour Unions," *The Globe and Mail*, May 11, 1987.

32. "B.C. Labour 'Time Bomb' Ticking," *Financial Post*, September 14, 1987.

33. "An Analysis of the Proposed College of Teachers," memorandum, BCTF, April 1987, p. 2.

34. L. Slotnick, "General Strike to Fight Labour Laws Gaining Favour Among B.C. Unions," *The Globe and Mail*, May 12, 1987.

35. Quoted in S. Morison, "Teacher Power Face-off," *Western Report*, September 14, 1987, p. 36.

36. A. Finkel, in the *Athabasca University Magazine*; Special Supplement, May 1987, p. 39. See also L. Slotnick, "Alberta's Labour Movement May Reap Gainer's Reward," *The Globe and Mail*, December 20, 1986.

37. See ILO *Official Bulletin*, cited in previous chapter; and D. Fudge, "ILO Condemns Restrictive Labour Laws in Canada," *Canadian Labour*, January 1986, p. 15.
38. J. Clark, "Labour Scene," *Journal of Commerce*, June 15, 1987. See also J. Bagnall, "Construction Workers Lead Labour's Retreat," *Financial Post*, March 1, 1986.
39. "Province Asserts Right to Define Labour Status," *The Globe and Mail*, September 25, 1984.
40. See L. Slotnick, "Labour Board Rankles Saskatchewan Unions," *The Globe and Mail*, April 18, 1986.
41. R. Sass, "Department of Labour: What's in a Name," *The Labour Reporter*, Saskatchewan Federation of Labour, February 1987.
42. In the most recent round of pay negoitations, the government did not in fact exercise its right to set wages in the second and third years of the agreement—as part of securing a settlement. Nevertheless, the wage increases explicitly guaranteed by the government from 3.5 per cent in 1986 to 4.5 per cent in 1988— fell well within the austerity guidelines proclaimed by the Treasury Board at the outset of negotiations. See L. Bissonnette, "Bourassa Triumphs Over Unions," *The Globe and Mail*, January 3, 1987.
43. CUPE, *The Public Employee*, Summer 1986, p. 13- 14.
44. L. Bissonnette, op. cit.
45. Monique Simard, CNTU Vice-President, quoted in the *Montreal Gazette*, November 12, 1986.
46. Federation of Engineering and Scientific Association's Newsletter, June 1986, p. 5. The report was endorsed by the unions although, not without some reservations. See *Canadian Labour*, February 1986, p. 7.
47. M. Tremblay, "Labour is Worried that Good Times May Not Last Long," *The Globe and Mail*, September 18, 1986.
48. *Canadian Labour*, (July/August 1985).
49. K. Stickney, "Nova Scotia's CLMB confident it can extend control," *Daily Commercial News*, April 3, 1987.
50. P. Gard, "Newfoundland begins labour practices overhaul," *Financial Times*, May 3, 1986.
51. Quoted in *The Globe and Mail*, December 27, 1984
52. A thoughtful discussion of this problem is offered by A. Forrest, "Bargaining Units Sans Bargaining Power," Proceedings of the 23rd Annual Meeting of the Canadian Industrial Relations Association, University of Manitoba, May 29-31, 1986. See also "First-Contract Arbitration Plan 'Tilts' Labour-business Relationship," *The Financial Post*, January 11, 1986.
53. See the *Financial Times*, September 9, 1986.
54. A. Rezori, "NAPE would have Accepted Labour Department's Proposal," *Evening Telegram*, September 18, 1986.
55. C. Finn, "A Political War, Says Peckford," *Evening Telegram*, September 16, 1986.
56. Quoted in *The Weekend Evening Telegram*, October 25, 1986.
57. P. Phillips, "Proposed Changes in Manitoba's Labour Laws: An Evaluation," unpublished ms., University of Manitoba, 1985, p. 10.
58. Labour Canada, "Highlights of Major Developments in Labour Legislation, 1984- 1985," *Labour Canada*, 1985, pp. 5-6. While this discussion is unclear on the point, it may be that a legal strike may require a vote of *all* employees and not just those who are union members.
59. See C. Gonick, "FOS—Splitting the Manitoba Labour Movement," *Canadian Dimension*, 21:6, October 1987; and L. Slotnick, "Manitoba's 'Final Offer' Splits Unions," *The Globe and Mail*, July 25, 1987.
60. It is not clear whether business' opposition is to the general thrust of the bill or merely the potential limit on the ability to lockout their employees.
61. See Bob White quote in "UAW Leader Urges Changes in First-contract Legislation," *The Globe and Mail*, April 2, 1986. As the title of this article suggests,

the unions thought that improvements in the act were possible, but the text shows that their reservations were few in number and marginal in nature.

62. See L. Slotnick, "Keeping Strike-breakers' jobs not Negotiable, OLRB Rules," *The Globe and Mail*, December 24, 1986.

63. See W. List, "Exit of Labour Official Part of a Liberal Trend," *The Globe and Mail*, August 12, 1986. The following draws largely on J. Deverell, "New Labour Minister Bill Wrye a Threat to NDP's Union Support," *The Toronto Star*, July 9, 1986. See also his "Labour Ministry Officials Sabotaging Laws to Protect Workers, Brief Says," *The Toronto Star*, September 28, 1986.

64. This thought was expressed by the Chairman of the Wellington County Board of Education, as quoted in M. Polanyi, "Everyone Will Lose in the Strike," *The Globe and Mail*, September 24, 1987. For the views of Ann Vanstone, see S. Contenta, "Boards Await Teacher 'Offer' that could Trigger New Talks," *The Toronto Star*, October 6, 1987.

65. An incisive critique of the Ontario Act is given by Isa Bakker, "Pay Equity in Ontario," *Canadian Dimension*, January 21, 1987, p. 4-5.

66. An excellent review of the pay equity experience to date in the federal and Quebec jurisdictions is provided by R. Warskett, "Valuing Women's Work: the Anatomy of a Policy," a proposal to the sshrc Strategic Grants Division: Thematic Programs 1987.

67. M. Cornish, "Equal Pay, Collective Bargaining and the Law," study prepared for Labour Canada, November 1986, p. 17.

68. Personal communication. Further evidence that this is already happening in Ontario, is reflected in Sara Growe, "Skirmishing Begins Over Equal Pay Law," *The Toronto Star*, December 13, 1987.

Chapter 6

1. J.C. Parrot, "An Interview," *Studies in Political Economy*, No. 11, Summer 1983, p. 61.

2. Gallup Canada Ltd., "Rise in Public Support for Right to Strike," *The Gallup Report*, April 23, 1987.

3. See Gene Swimmer, "The impact of the dispute resolution process on Canadian federal public service wage settlements," *Journal of Collective Negotiations*, 16:1, 1987.

4. C. Huxley, D. Kettner, and J. Struthers, "Is Canada's Experience Especially Instructive?" in S.M. Lipset (ed.), *Unions in Transition: Entering the Second Century*, (San Francisco: Institute for Contemporary Studies, 1986), p. 126.

5. For insightful surveys, see Bryan Palmer, *Working Class Experience: The Rise and Reconstitution of Canadian Labour, 1800-1980*, (Toronto: Butterworth, 1983), and Mike Davis, *Prisoners of the American Dream: Politics and Economy in the History of the US Working Class*, (London: Verso, 1986).

6. Marvin Gandall, "Labour in the Winter of '87," *Canadian Dimension*, February 1987, pp. 27-8. The data on wage rates in this paragraph are drawn primarily from *The Current Industrial Relations Scene in Canada, 1987*, Industrial Relations Centre, Queen's University, Reference Tables, pp. 597-8. Cf. M. Gunderson and N. Meltz, "Recent developments in the Canadian Industrial Relations System," Centre for Industrial Relations, University of Toronto, 1985; P. Benimadhu, "Management-Labour Relations Today: Tough Negotiations Ahead," *Canadian Business Review*, Summer 1987, pp. 21-4. P. Kumar, "Recent labour-management relations approaches in Canada," Industrial Relations Centre, Queen's University, 1987, esp. p. 13, n. 5.

7. For a detailed examination of the labour movement's response to "6 and 5," see R. Long, "Labour Struggles Within the Canadian State: Bill C-124 and the Labour

Response," M.A. Thesis, Department of Political Science, Carleton University, 1984.

8. See especially H. Glasbeek and M. Mandel, "The Legalisation of Politics: Legal Rights in the Charter of Rights and Freedoms," in R. Martin (ed.), *Critical Perspectives on the Constitution*, a special theme issue of *Socialist Studies: A Canadian Annual*, Vol. 2, 1984; and H. Glasbeek, "Workers of the World: Avoid the Charter of Rights," *Canadian Dimension*, April 1987, pp. 12-14.

9. Parrot, "An Interview," p. 60.

10. See Bryan Palmer, *Solidarity: Rise and Fall of an Opposition in British Columbia*, (Vancouver: New Star, 1987), who provides a strong defence of the potential efficacy of the general strike strategy derailed by the leadership. We take up this question below.

11. *Attorney General of British Columbia v. Ken Georgetti et al*, Supreme Court of British Columbia, Vancouver Registry, No. C872660, June 10, 1987.

12. See *Boycott Manual*, B.C. Federation of Labour, August 1987; S. Weatherbe, "Continuing furor over labour," *Western Report*, August 1987, p. 5.

13. Roy Haynes, "Looking Backward: One Year Later," *New Directions: Life and Politics in B.C.*, Vol. 3, no. 2, November/December 1987, pp. 27-8.

14. A remarkable view of the different strategies advanced is afforded by *The Bill 19 Letters: Correspondence between the Confederation of Canadian Unions and the B.C. Federation of Labour and Premier Vander Zalm*, prepared and released by the Confederation of Canadian Unions, New Westminster, B.C., 1987. Cf. Lorne Slotnick, "General strike to fight labor laws gaining favor among B.C. unions," *The Globe and Mail*, May 12, 1987; and R. Mickleburgh, "B.C. Labor 'Time Bomb' Ticking," *Financial Times*, September 14, 1987.

15. Parrot, "An Interview," p. 67.

16. An excellent discussion is offered by A. Cumsille, et al., "Triple Oppression: Immigrant Women in the labour Force," in L. Briskin and L. Yanz (ed.), *Union Sisters: Women in the Labour Movement*, (Toronto: Women's Educational Press, 1983), pp. 212-21.

17. Heather Jon Maroney, "Feminism at Work," *New Left Review*, No. 141, September/October, 1983, p. 64. Reprinted as Chapter Five in J. Maroney, M. Luxton (eds.), *Feminism and Political Economy: Women's Work, Women's Struggles*, (Toronto: Methuen, 1987).

18. Linda Briskin, "Interview," in *Labour*, a special supplement of the Athabasca University Magazine in honour of the 75th anniversary of the Alberta Federation of Labour, Vol. 10, No. 5, 1987, p. 13. See also Briskin's "Women's Challenge to Organized Labour," in *Union Sisters*, pp. 260-71.

19. *Re Lavigne and OPSEU*, 55 *Ontario Reports* (2d), 1987, pp. 454-521. Also see Glasbeek, "Workers of the World;" J. Clancy et al., *The Trial of the Century, All For One: Arguments from OPSEU*, (Toronto: 1985); L. Slotnick, "Union dues case: just how far does it reach?" *The Globe and Mail*, July 14, 1987; W. List, "Labour movement discovers Charter is a two-edged sword," *The Glove and Mail: Report on Business*, July 19, 1987; J. Bagnall, "Labor not so worried by dues ruling," *The Financial Post*, August 2, 1987.

LEGISLATION AND ORDERS SUSPENDING THE RIGHT TO STRIKE 1950-1987

A. Federal Back-to-work Legislation
1. The Maintenance of Railway Operation Act (August 30, 1950).
2. The British Columbia Coast Steamship Service Act (July 25, 1958).
3. The Railway Operation Continuation Act (December 2, 1960).
4. The Maritime Transportation Unions Trustee Act (October 18, 1963).
5. The St. Lawrence Ports Working Conditions Act (July 14, 1966)
6 The Maintenance of Railway Operation Act, 1966 (September 1, 1966).
7. The St. Lawrence Ports Operations Act (July 7, 1972).
8. The West Coast Ports Operations Act (September 1, 1972).
9. The Maintenance of Railway Operations Act, 1973 (September 1, 1973).
10. The West Coast Grain Handling Operations Act, 1974 (October 10, 1974).
11. The West Coast Ports Operations Act, 1975 (March 24, 1975).
12. The St. Lawrence Ports Operations Act, 1975 (April 24, 1975).
13. The Port of Halifax Operations Act (October 22, 1976)
14. The Air Traffic Control Services Continuation Act (August 10, 1977).
15. The Postal Services Continuation Act (October 18, 1978).
16. The Shipping Continuation Act (October 24, 1978).
17. The West Coast Ports Operations Act, 1982 (November 4, 1982).
18. The Maintenance of Ports Operations Act, 1986 (November 18, 1986).
19. Maintenance of Railway Operations Act, 1987 (August 28, 1987).
20. Postal Services Continuation Act, 1987 (October 16, 1987).

B. Provincial Back-to-work Legislation
1. Newfoundland: The Trade Union (Emergency Provisions) Act, 1959 (March 6, 1959).
2. Ontario: The Ontario Hydro-Employees' Union Dispute Act, 1965 (June 10, 1965).
3. Ontario: The Toronto Hydro-Employees' Union Dispute Act, 1965 (June 10, 1965).

4. Quebec: An Act to amend the Transportation Board Act (October 22, 1965).
5. Saskatchewan: The Essential Services Emergency Act, 1966 (September 8, 1966).
6. Newfoundland: The Hospital Employees (Employment) Act, 1966-67 (January 27, 1967).
7. Quebec: An Act to ensure for children the right to education and to institute a new schooling collective agreement plan (February 17, 1967).
8. Quebec: An Act to ensure for users the resumption of the normal services of the Montreal Transportation Commission (October 21, 1967).
9. Quebec: An Act to ensure the protection of police and fire services to the citizens of Montreal (October 7, 1969).
10. Quebec: An Act to ensure the right to education to the pupils of the Commission scolaire régionale de Chambly (October 23, 1969).
11. Quebec: An Act respecting the construction industry (August 8, 1970).
12. Quebec: An Act to ensure resumption of services in the public sector (April 21, 1972).
13. Quebec: An Act respecting the essential services of Hydro-Quebec (November 15, 1972).
14. Ontario: The Elevator Constructor Unions Disputes Act, 1973 (March 22, 1973).
15. Ontario: The York County Board of Education Teachers' Dispute Act, 1974 (March 15, 1974).
16. Quebec: An Act respecting the placing of the "International Union of Elevator Constructors, locals 89 and 101" under trusteeship (July 17, 1974).
17. British Columbia: Essential Services Continuation Act (August 9, 1974)
18. Ontario: The Toronto Transit Commission Labour Disputes Settlement Act, 1974 (August 31, 1974).
19. British Columbia: Elevator Construction Industry Labour Disputes Act (November 26, 1974).
20. Saskatchewan: The Maintenance of Operations of Saskatchewan Power Corporation Act, 1975 (January 15, 1975).
21. Quebec: An Act to ensure users the resumption of the normal services of the Montreal Urban Community Transit Commission (September 27, 1975).
22. British Columbia: Collective Bargaining Continuation Act (October 7, 1975).
23. Ontario: The Metropolitan Toronto Boards of Education and Teachers Disputes Act, 1976 (January 16, 1976).
24. Ontario: The Kirkland Lake Board of Education and Teachers Dispute Act, 1976 (March 11, 1976).
25. Quebec: An Act respecting the maintaining of services in the sector of education and repealing a certain legislative provision (April 9, 1976)
26. Ontario: The Central Algoma Board of Education and Teachers Dispute Act, 1976 (April 14, 1976).
27. Ontario: The Sault Ste. Marie Board of Education and Teachers Dispute Act, 1976 (April 14, 1976).
28. Ontario: The Windsor Board of Education and Teachers Dispute Act, 1976 (May 7, 1976).
29. British Columbia: Hospital Services Collective Agreement Act (June 9, 1976).
30. British Columbia: Railway and Ferries Bargaining Assistance Act (June 14, 1976).
31. Quebec: An Act respecting health services in certain establishments (July 24, 1976).
32. Ontario: The Toronto Transit Commission Labour Disputes Settlement Act, 1978 (September 13, 1978).
33. British Columbia: West Kootenay Schools Collective Bargaining Assistance Act (December 9, 1978).
34. Quebec: An Act respecting proposals to employees in education, social affairs and civil service sectors (November 12, 1979)

35. Quebec: An Act to ensure the maintaining of electrical services and to provide the conditions of employment of the employees of Hydro-Quebec (December 18, 1979).
36. Quebec: An Act to ensure the resumption of certain services of the City of Montreal and the Communauté urbaine de Montréal (March 24, 1980).
37. Saskatchewan: The Maintenance of Operations of Dairy Producers Co-operative Limited and Palm Dairies Limited Act (May 9, 1980).
38. Quebec: An Act respecting certain disputes between teachers and school boards (October 24, 1980).
39. Ontario: The Leeds and Grenville County Board of Education and Teachers Dispute Act, 1981 (July 3, 1981).
40. Newfoundland: The Essential Health Services Act (November 6, 1981).
41. Quebec: An Act respecting the transit service of the Commission de transport de la Communauté urbaine de Montréal (January 15, 1982).
42. Alberta: Health Services Continuation Act (March 10, 1982).
43. Saskatchewan: The Labour-Management Dispute (Temporary Provisions) Act (March 26, 1982).
44. New Brunswick: An Act to Ensure Resumption and Continuation of Certain Non-teaching Services in the Public Service (April 14, 1982).
45. Saskatchewan: The Cancer-Foundation (Maintenance of Operations) Act (August 20, 1982).
46. Quebec: An Act to ensure the resumption of public transit service in the territory of the Communauté urbaine de Québec (November 6, 1982).
47. Quebec: An act to ensure the resumption of services in the schools and colleges in the public sector (February 17, 1983).
48. Quebec: An Act to ensure the resumption of public transit service in the territory of the Communauté urbaine de Montréal (May 12, 1983).
49. British Columbia: Pulp and Paper Collective Bargaining Assistance Act (April 3, 1984).
50. Saskatchewan: The Dairy Workers (Maintenance of Operations) Act (April 9, 1984).
51. Ontario: Toronto Transit Commission, Gray Coach Lines, Limited and Go Transit Labour Disputes Settlement Act, 1984 (August 29, 1984).
52. British Columbia: Metro Transit Collective Bargaining Assistance Act (September 13, 1984).
53. Ontario: Colleges of Applied Arts and Technology Labour Dispute Settlement Act, 1984 (November 9, 1984).
54. Quebec: An Act respecting the continuation of services by and conditions of employment of ambulance technicians in administrative region 6A (greater Montreal) (December 20, 1984).
55. British Columbia: British Columbia Railway Dispute Settlement Act (May 16, 1985).
56. Ontario: Wellington County Board of Education and Teachers Dispute Settlement Act, 1985 (November 26, 1985)
57. Saskatchewan: The SGEU Dispute Settlement Act (January 31, 1986).
58. Quebec: An Act respecting the resumption of transportation service in the territory of certain school boards (March 27, 1986).
59. Ontario: Wheel-Trans Labour Dispute Settlement Act, 1986 (April 25, 1986).
60. Quebec: An Act to ensure the resumption of construction work (June 17, 1986).
61. Quebec: An Act to ensure that essential services are maintained in the health and social services sector (November 11, 1986).
62. Quebec: An Act respecting the resumption of certain services of the University of Québec at Montreal (May 7, 1987)

C. Orders Suspending the Right to Strike or to Lockout

Alberta
Suspension of the right to strike under section 148 of the Labour Relations Act (strike dates in parentheses)

1. Bow Valley School Authorities Association and Alberta Teachers Federation (November 29 - December 20, 1971).
2. Elevator Companies and International Union of Elevator Constructors (October 5, 1972 - March 25, 1973).
3. Southern Alberta School Authorities Association and Alberta Teachers Association (March 12 - April 2, 1973).
4. Alberta Hospitals Association and Alberta Association of Registered Nurses (July 4 - July 9, 1977).
5. Edmonton School Board District No. 7 and Alberta Teachers' Association (September 7 - September 20, 1978).
6. Alberta Hospitals Association and United Nurses Association (April 18 - April 28, 1980).
7. Calgary School District No. 19 and Alberta Teachers Association (May 27 - September 29, 1980).

New Brunswick
Suspension of the right to strike or to lockout under subsections 80(4), 91(5) and 91(6) of the Industrial Relations Act.

1. Bathurst Police (July 11, 1979).
2. Moncton Police (May 14, 1985).
3. Saint John Police (May 17, 1985).
4. Chatham Police (June 13, 1985).

British Columbia
Suspension of the Right to Strike under Essential Services Disputes Act (1977)

1. Esquimalt Police (February 5, 1985).
2. Victoria Police (March 4, 1985).
3. Oak Bay Police (August 5, 1985).
4. Health Care Workers (August 5, 1986).

Quebec
Suspension of the right to strike under section 111.0.24 of the Labour Code (1982)

1. Union of maintenance employees for the Montreal South Shore Transit Commission (February 16, 1986).
2. Blue collar workers employed by the City of Montreal (March 19, 1986).
3. Maintenance employees of the Montreal Urban Community Transit Commission (May 4, 1987).

Legislation Amending Trade Union Rights:
June 1982—December 1987

I. **Temporary Restrictive Measures**
A. Federal
- Bill C-124, Public Sector Compensation Restraint Act (August 4, 1982)[1]
- SOR/83-812, Ontario and Nova Scotia Contracts Fair Wages and Hours of Work Exception Order (October 26, 1983) (gazetted)
- SOR/84-361, Prince Edward Island Fair Wages and Hours of Work Exception Order (May 15, 1984) (gazetted)

B. Provincial and Territorial
Prince Edward Island
- Bill 39, Compensation Review Act (June 23, 1983)
Nova Scotia
- Bill 71, Public Sector Compensation Act (June 6, 1983)
Quebec
- Bill 70, An Act Respecting Remuneration in the Public Sector (June 23, 1982)
- Bill 105, An Act Respecting the Conditions of Employment in the Public Sector (December 11, 1982)
- Bill 111, An Act to Ensure the Resumption of Services in the Schools and Colleges in the Public Sector (February 17, 1983)
Ontario
- Bill 179, Inflation Restraint Act, 1982 (December 16, 1982)
- Bill 111, Public Sector Prices and Compensation Review Act, 1983 (December 16, 1983)
Alberta
- Bill 53, Construction Industry Collective Bargaining Act (June 17, 1987)
British Columbia
- Bill 28, Compensation Stabilization Act (June 25, 1982)

Yukon Territory
• Bill 17, Public Sector Compensation Restraint (Yukon) Act (December 9, 1982)

II. Permanent Restrictive Measures

A. Federal
• Bill C-45, Parliamentary Employment and Staff Relations Act (June 27, 1986)

B. Provincial and Territorial
Newfoundland
• Bill 59, An Act to Amend the Public Service (Collective Bargaining) Act, 1973 (May 31, 1983)
• Bill 37, An Act to Amend the Labour Standards Act (December 19, 1984)
Nova Scotia
• Reg. 17/83, Amendment to the General Regulations Under the Labour Standards Code, (February 24, 1983) (gazetted)
• Bill 91, An Act to Amend Chapter 19 of the Acts of 1972, the Trade Union Act (May 26, 1986)
New Brunswick
• Bill 50, An Act to Amend the Industrial Relations Act (February 17, 1983)
Quebec
• Bill 68, An Act to Amend Various Legislation Respecting Pension Plans (June 23, 1982)
• Bill 72, An Act to Amend the Labour Code, the Code of Civil Procedure and Other Legislation (June 23, 1982)
• Bill 37, An Act respecting the process of negotiation of the collective agreements in the public and parapublic sectors (June 19, 1985)
• Bill 119, An Act to amend the Act respecting labour relations in the construction industry (December 17, 1986)
Ontario
• Bill 75, An Act to Amend the Labour Relations Act (June 16, 1984)
Saskatchewan
• Bill 45, The Labour-Management Dispute (Temporary Provisions) Act (March 26, 1982)
• Bill 104, An Act to Amend the Trade Union Act (June 17, 1983)
• Bill 24, An Act to Repeal the Construction Industry Labour Relations Act (December 12, 1983)
• Reg. 16/84, Public Service Amendment Regulation Under the Public Service Act (March 9, 1984)
Alberta
• Bill 11, Health Services Continuation Act (March 10, 1982)
• Bill 44, Labour Statutes Amendment Act, 1983 (June 6, 1983)
• Bill 93, Police Officers Collective Bargaining Act (November 30, 1983)
• Bill 110, Labour Relations Amendment Act (November 30, 1983)
• Bill 30, Public Service Employee Relations Amendment Act (June 5, 1985)
• Bill 60, Labour Code, introduced (June 17, 1987)
British Columbia
• Bill 50, Labour Code Amendment Act, 1982 (Proclaimed August 4, 1982)
• Bill 11, Compensation Stabilization Amendment Act, 1983 (October 21, 1983)
• Bill 3, Public Sector Restraint Act (October 21, 1983)
• Bill 16, The Employment Development Act (October 21, 1983)
• Bill 26, Employment Standards Amendment Act, 1983 (October 21, 1983)
• Reg. 247/83, Proclamation of section 4 of the Public Service Labour Relations Amendment Act, 1975 (S.B.C. -1975 c.61) (July 12, 1983) (gazetted)
• Bill 28, Labour Code Amendment, 1984 (May 16, 1984)

- Bill 32, Compensation Stabilization Amendment Act, 1985 (June 3, 1985)
- Bill 19, Industrial Relations Reform Act (June 26, 1987)
- Bill 20, Teaching Profession Act (June 26, 1987)

North West Territories
- Reg. R-034, A Regulation to Amend the Labour Relations Act and various other Acts of the Legislature (June 24, 1983)

III. Reform Measures

A. Federal
- Bill C-34, An Act to Amend the Canada Labour Code and the Financial Administration Act (June 29, 1984) [2]

B. Provincial and Territorial

Newfoundland
- Bill 14, An Amendment to the Labour Relations Act (June 28, 1985)
- Bill 15, An Act to Amend the Public Service (Collective Bargaining) Act, 1973 (June 28, 1985)

New Brunswick
- Bill 28, An Act to Amend the Employment Standards Act (June 18, 1986)

Prince Edward Island
- Bill 47, An Act to Amend the Labour Act (1) (May 14, 1987)
- Bill 55, An Act to Amend the Labour Act (2) (May 14, 1987)
- Bill 75, Pay Equity Act, introduced (April 28, 1987)

Ontario
- Bill 62, An Act to Amend the Labour Relations Act (June 21, 1983)
- Bill 65, Labour Relations Amendment Act, 1986 (May 26, 1986)
- Bill 154, Pay Equity Act (June 29, 1987)

Manitoba
- Bill 40, An Act to Amend the Labour Relations Act (June 30, 1982)
- Bill 22, An Act to Amend the Labour Relations Act and various other Acts of the Legislature (June 29, 1984)
- Bill 53, Pay Equity Act (July 11, 1985)
- Bill 74, Equal Rights Statute Amendment Act (July 11, 1985)
- Bill 61, An Act to Amend the Labour Relations Act (July 16, 1987)

Yukon
- Bill 99, Human Rights Act (February 12, 1987)

1. Date given is the date of Royal Assent unless otherwise noted.
2. Only section V was actually proclaimed.

Garamond Books:

- Argue, Gannagé, Livingstone: *Working People and Hard Times: Canadian Perspectives*
- Basranand Hay: *Political Economy of Agriculture in Western Canada*
- Bolaria and Li (eds): *Racial Oppression in Canada* (2nd. ed.)
- Brickey and Comack (eds): *The Social Basis of Law*
- Brym (ed): *The Structure of the Canadian Capitalist Class*
- Burrill and McKay: *People, Resources and Power*
- Cantelon and Hollands: *Leisure, Sport and Working Class Cultures*
- Centennial College English Faculty Association: *Writing for the Job*
- Dickinson and Russell: *Family, Economy and State*
- Gruneau: *Popular Cultures and Political Practices*
- Henderson: *The Future on the Table: From Liberalism to the Challenge of Feminism*
- Knuttila: *State Theories: From Liberalism to the Challenge of Feminism*
- Livingstone (ed): *Critical Pedagogy & Cultural Power*
- Moscovitch and Albert (eds): *The Benevolent State: The Growth of the Welfare State*
- Niosi: *Canadian Multinationals*
- Olsen: *Industrial Change and Labour Adjustment in Sweden and Canada*
- Panitch & Swartz: *The Assault on Trade Union Freedoms* (2nd. ed.)
- Young (ed): *Breaking the Mosaic: Ethnic Identities in Canadian Schooling*

The Network Basic Series

- Acheson, Frank and Frost: *Industrialization and Underdevelopment in the Maritimes, 1880-1930*
- Armstrong and Armstrong: *Theorizing Women's Work*
- Armstrong et al: *Feminist Marxism or Marxist Feminism*
- Buchbinder et al: *Who's On Top: The Politics of Heterosexuality*
- Burstyn and Smith: *Women, Class, Family and the State*; Intro by Ng
- Cohen: *Free Trade and the Future of Women's Work*
- Duffy, Mandell and Pupo: *Few Choices: Women, Work and Home*
- Lacombe: *Ideology and Public Policy: The Case Against Pornography*
- Livingstone: *Social Crisis and Schooling*
- Lowe and Northcott: *Under Pressure: a Study of Job Stress*
- Luxton and Rosenberg: *Through the Kitchen Window: the Politics of Home and Family*
- Newson and Buchbinder: *The University Means Business*
- Ng: *The Politics of Community Services*
- Veltmeyer: *The Canadian Class Structure*
- Veltmeyer: *Canadian Corporate Power*
- White: *Law, Capitalism and the Right to Work*

Garamond Press, 67A Portland St., Toronto, Ont., M5V 2M9
(416) 597-0246